Adapting to Digital Transformation

Design sensible SLAs for modern IT

PRAFULL VERMA
MOHAN KEWALRAMANI AND
KALYAN KUMAR

ISBN-13: 978-0692889169
ISBN-10: 0692889167

March 2018

ACKNOWLEDGMENTS

Immediately after publishing my first book "Process Excellence for IT Operations", I established a charter to add a few more books related to IT Service Management. Since then, I have added five more books, but this book was not in my original charter and suddenly ideated when one of my colleagues Srivatchan Rajaraman argued that Service Level Management is a subject that deserves its own dedicated publication. After an initial debate, I agreed, and the project was kicked off. I would therefore like to thank Srivatchan for providing an effective trigger.

Like all other books, this contains lots of my own points of view; largely an education and some guidance to apply that education. The audience does not need to be technology savvy at all.

After a long tenure in working on different technologies, I developed a strong inclination to service management at the functional layer of technology (the layer that has touch points with technology; it is the interface between the business purpose of the technology and the technology itself). There was a vacuum of professionals in this area. This vacuum is now being rapidly filled because of the proliferation of technology in every aspect of the business.

All previous books provided "functional guidance" but this book is a step further away from technology and looks at purely the commercial aspects of service management. I hope you will get value from reading it.

Like all other books, the support and cooperation of my wife Annie and daughter Naomi was an important motivation for me to complete this project.

Prafull Verma

I would like to thank my wife Maisa, who has made this and everything else possible for me. She has truly been the enabler for everything that I have experienced, learnt and achieved. Also, my two boys, Zaahid and Aariz, for always keeping me grounded.

Everything that I have learnt, has been at the time and expense of all the customers that I have had the opportunity to work with, I sincerely thank them, as without them, none of this would have been possible. Last, but not the least, all of my colleagues in HCL, who I have learnt a lot from.

Mohan Kewalramani

Ever Since my exposure to the world of "everything as a service" delivery models, I have recognized the struggles that most clients have been through. Infact, we came across them even in the traditional legacy world. It is an important aspect to get right or can have an immediate impact on relationships with the supplier base.

I would like to thank my wife Zulfia and Son Azlan who have given me the space and time out of their share to enable me to write this book and always inspire me in pushing the limits and also acting like a sounding board to simplifying my thoughts.

Kalyan Kumar

FOREWORD

Businesses across industries stand at an inflection point today due to far reaching disruption fueled by what I call the three elephants in the room: Automation, Cloud and Digitalization. The momentum of change, fueled by an explosion of data and connected devices, software defined infrastructure, cloud-enabled as-a-service and experience & outcome driven digital platforms, is forcing enterprises to reimagine their businesses and rewire it for success in the new world. The models in which IT services are sourced have changed, dependencies between providers still exist to deliver an aggregated end to end service. There is however a tendency for organizations to still measure the performance of services delivered using the same service level criteria as traditionally delivered services, this also requires a revision.

It is a common misconception that an SLA framework defines the actual level of service that will be delivered and sets the expectations of both parties of what "should" be delivered. On several occasions, I have seen this cause more harm than good when crafted incorrectly. Poorly designed SLAs have the ability to get a supplier to focus their efforts on the inconsequential, while ignoring the critical. This usually happens when financial penalties are at stake and used as the stick to beat the supplier. These agreements tend to take a more legal connotation and ignore the spirit and intent that they were meant to drive.

Prafull Verma, Mohan Kewalramani and Kalyan Kumar, all colleagues of mine at HCL Technologies, have advised numerous clients on their SLA models and constructs. They have together probably come across most SLA anomalies, unreasonable asks and also have had to deal with dependencies of different partners in a multi supplier ecosystem with little to no correlation between the SLAs among these parties. They have had to steer and guide the clients as well as our delivery organizations through these tricky discussions and a lot of their guidance in this book is based on those experiences.

I doubt there is a single magic formula for the perfect SLA framework, this book provides pragmatic and practical advice on common pitfalls when designing, measuring and agreeing SLAs and will guide you on how to get to a sensible place. The authors provide considerations for both the buyers as well as the suppliers of IT services. It addresses the changes required in mind-set due to shifts in technology and delivery methods as well as tackles more subjective issues like user experience, personalization in a largely commoditized industry and how to address SLA discussions for these. It is an excellent read for anyone that is required to drive a long term successful business relationship, whatever that may be.

C Vijayakumar
President & Chief Executive Officer
HCL Technologies

TABLE OF CONTENT

1 Introduction

It wasn't that long ago that Service Level Agreement's (SLAs) for IT services came into existence. They evolved from the SLAs of telecommunication services in the early 1980's and proliferated with the IT helpdesk in the late 1980's. The need of a formal SLA was never really felt before that. While telecom SLAs were focused mostly on the quality of the data communication services, helpdesk SLAs were multidimensional in nature. As I recall, the formalization of an SLA for IT services started with the best practice promoted by the Helpdesk Institute in the early 1990s. This too was only focused on the SLAs for support services. With the widespread adoption of the ITIL framework and best practices, Service Level Agreement's became a prominent component in the service management domain.

A SLA is a formal, written and signed *agreement* between a service provider and the service consumer or buyer which lists agreed aspects of the service - quality, availability, responsibilities, etc. We shouldn't however confuse an SLA with other published specifications or expectations set by manufacturers of products or service delivery organizations. A 'product specification' for example describes the features or maximum capable capacity of the product; a warranty in its purest form is a component of a contract but generally means a guarantee or promise accompanying a product so that the manufacturer assures a consumer with whom they have no direct contractual relationship. This is typically used for products you buy from stores, online, retailers or resellers and set the boundaries of how and typically the length of time a product is expected to function as intended; if it doesn't, then the assurance is that the manufacturer will provide support, which may be in the form of some repair or replacement. Utility of a service describes how useful something is in relation to what it is designed for. In economic terms, it can also refer to the satisfaction received from consuming goods or a service. A service warranty describes the maintenance support provided and also sometimes denotes an extended warranty, which can be purchased at an additional cost, extends the period that a manufacturer will assure intended usage and provide repair or replacement support. So, there are several terms that describe the capability and features of products, how long you can be assured they will function and how the manufacturer will support them. These of course then go into a deeper labyrinth of limited warranty, international warranty and the fine print which states that if you were to purchase an extended warranty, it overlaps the manufacturer's warranty.

IT Service Operations revolve around SLAs

The intention of agreeing an SLA is quite clear. It is to ensure that both parties understand exactly what level of service and availability will be provided as part of the relationship. They are negotiated prior to a contract is signed. If the services are provided by the same legal entity, this may not be a legal document or formal contract, but you still need a formal agreement. However, when these are agreed with an external supplier, this usually always forms part of a legal contract. As you can imagine, at that stage, when a contract is being negotiated or has yet to be signed, the supplier tries extremely hard to make a good impression on the client. They want the client to understand and feel that the supplier is the best partner to work with. I am not trying to imply that the supplier is not good or deceiving the client in any way. They could be the best and most appropriate supplier for that client in the market. This is akin to courting your partner and we all know that you always put your best face forward to make a good impression. However, marriage is another game altogether. Again, not that the person is wrong for you, the marriage may be very happy and last until death do you part, but divorce and unhappy marriages are also equally common. I am certain that unhappy couples also had a very successful courtship!

SLAs in a commercial relationship are a set of commitments and measures. It is like agreeing with your partner in writing how you will measure your marriage, what they can expect from you and how you will be punished if you don't perform. Thinking aloud, this may not be a bad thing after all. The point I am trying to make is that the contracting period is like "courting" and the measurements and commitments agreed at that time are also done with a very positive intent and spirit. The supplier wants the client to feel confident that they are making the right decision in partnering with them. There is however a much murkier side to what actually happens when the contract is signed, and the relationship progresses into a daily grind. The focus of running operations is usually on meeting the agreed SLAs. It is usually not on providing the best service, irrespective of SLA achievement. The assumption is that if the SLAs are green, then life is good, and the relationship is healthy, although this may not always be the case. Many of you would have heard about the watermelon effect, which is green from the outside, but red inside. This is also true for many of the supplier-client relationships. The SLAs paint a story of great service and in line with the agreement as they all appear green, while the perception of the service received by the end user can very easily be red. I have provided some more real-life examples of this further in the book. By developing sensible SLAs you can minimize the scope of the watermelon effect. The underlying issue is that the intent and spirit in which the SLAs were written and agreed are usually ignore and it all comes down to hard numbers and a rigid measurement methodology. I do agree that it would be unfair to generalize and claim that every supplier-client relationship will suffer from this and that all suppliers provide a bad service. Just like there are many happy and successful marriages, many a business relationship thrive for years with both sides extremely happy. But, there are unhappy relationships too.

The other issue is our general mentality as people and the influence of acceptable and generally followed western practices. I was in Vegas earlier this year. As exciting as that sounds, it wasn't to party and gamble my savings away, it was to attend a conference. On a road leading up to the hotel, there were several billboards lining the street. Each and every one of them was advertising the services of an injury lawyer that said if you had an accident or injury, then to call their number. There were no billboards for the medical care or fantastic facilities in the area. Instead of focusing on the recovery after an accident, the action promoted is get compensation. We have the same issue in IT operations. If there is an issue with not achieving the expected level of service or if there is an outage, a lot of focus shifts to penalties and rebates on service charges.

You will also notice that in reference to SLA documents several terms are used when referring to the role that consumes the service. Confusing as they may be, it is important to distinguish between the different terms:

- **Customer:** Someone who "buys" or "pays" for the products or services. Now this could have an interpretation that the "finance or procurement" team is always the Customer as they pay the bill. However, the Customer of an IT Service Provider is the person or group who defines and agrees to the service level targets. This could be a business relationship manager or a business head. There will also be several IT services that will be provided by internal teams and there may be no direct payment for the services, but a "show-back" or even just apportioning the costs of the service across several business groups that consume the service.
- **User:** Someone who "consumes" or "uses" the product or services. They could be a very different group from the person who "buys" the service, i.e. the Customer. Users are also referred to as end user in IT environment. The Service desk often refers to end users as customers

The above are very commonly understood terms in the industry, as they are defined by ITIL and familiar to most IT folks. However, when dealing with SLA documents, which have more of an underlying legal tone and could be part of a larger "contract". It is also quite common to come across the following terms, which also have similar meanings:

- **Client:** An industry specific term for a person that buys the service. You have probably come across the term "client" in the legal profession and have definitely heard it in the movies when they refer to the "attorney client privilege"; the client being the person the lawyer is representing and paying for the service. Of course, if it is pro-bono or free, then the client is receiving the services at no cost to them directly but lets not confuse this anymore.
- **Consumer:** This is another term for the person that uses or consumes the service. It is commonly used in the retail or even utility industry.

This book will provide guidance and some insight into developing sensible SLAs to give the relationship the best chance of success.

In IT, the most discussed and common SLAs relate to support of the service and the user, therefore it would be worthwhile to discuss the trends around assisted service provided by the Service Desk.

1.1 Is assisted support vanishing?

Service catalog and do-it-yourself

We see a rising trend of "serve yourself" in many industries. Digitalization of processes has made it easier to enable the user to fulfil several, if not all steps in the transaction. This is no longer just limited to requesting for a service by filling and submitting a form. Everyone is familiar with checking in for a flight, which earlier was only done at the airport by the airline agent. Now, you just go to the desk to drop your bags. There are certain budget airlines that charge you if you show up at the desk and ask an agent to process your check-in and print your boarding passes. This is an aggressive push towards self-service. I was surprised to notice at one of the largest fast food chains (yes, the one with the golden arches), that they now have a touch screen for you to order your own food instead of going to the counter. Assisted support is already reducing and will likely be a thing of the past very soon. It will be an exception. This is a growing trend in the IT services industry too. With the maturity of cloud services, automation, the dependency on manually performed tasks by support resources is already on the decline. In many cases, assisted support would either not be economically viable or become irrelevant due to self-healing characteristics of the service. Self-service is a high value component in every catalogued service. Besides this, self-service is getting much easier to enable as technology has come a very long way over the past 10 years. Everyone has access to a smartphone and computer. We see this in the personal banking and airline industry. Do you recall when was the last time you called the bank or the airline to process a transaction? There is very little personal banking that you cannot do from anywhere on your smartphone. Why can this not happen in enterprise IT? The new generation workforce, also referred to as "born digital" are very accustomed to using the latest technology, they have grown up with it and they prefer self-service anyway. Of course, some form of assisted service would exist, but the assistance would likely be delivered by artificial intelligent machines and not by a human.

Customized service is out, standardized service with personalization is in;

Customized and tailor-made service is vanishing, even though the concept of good customer service is growing stronger, but in a slightly very different manner. The customer service provided is directly proportional to the value of the customer to the business. It is directly related to how much money you generate for the business. Look at the personal banking industry. In several banks, if you have a large amount of money saved or are successful enough to have a large salary coming into your account each month, you are assigned a "personal banking advisor". This doesn't mean you get any extra from the bank, but it is an elevated form of support and attention. The same level of service isn't provided to all customers of the bank. In the airline industry, loyalty schemes are popular and the more you fly with an airline *(equating to you spending more money with the airline)*, you move up tiers and get to avail of better services and facilities. Everybody who buys a ticket *(and isn't offloaded)* will board the plane, but the ones that spend the most money with the airline, board first. It is not just the most expensive class that board first, this is true even for economy class, because regular fliers who spend large sums of money with the airline, get the opportunity to be first in the queue as well. So, the overall perceived level of customer service may be increasing, especially with everything moving to a digital platform and systems now being able to analyze all our spending habits, where we buy from, how much and how often, but it is the concept of "customized service" that is quickly vanishing. Look at the experience of buying from a local shop compared to a large grocery chain. In the good old days, the local shop owner knew you and your family personally, knew of every death and birth in the community and would even maintain a log book of credit to customers. This is in stark contrast to shopping at a large grocery chain or supermarket. The customer service you receive may be better, and the personalization you receive is dictated by the analytics engine they use. It is very difficult, if not impossible to understand every persons preferences, unless of course you equate customization to be the few items that you can put a check box into about time zone preferences or how you want to be addressed or if you want to receive email notifications. The only thing you really do is personalize the interface or the medium of consuming the service. The reality is that customized service is a big burden on the service provider. I was on a flight from LA to London last summer and was having a conversation with the stewardess. I thought they all preferred to serve passengers in first or business class, as the numbers were so much smaller than in economy. Once your rounds of drinks and meals are done, you can relax. This ought to be much quicker and less work in the front cabins, then in cattle class. But to my surprise, worse to be in business or first starting from LA, because the level of attention and customized service desired is very high, they can all be eating at different times. After all, everyone feels they are from Hollywood!

It is important to understand that every user is unique. He or she can produce a unique problem depending upon the way they use the product or service. You can make every computer behave in an identical manner by using the same brand, model, configuration of hardware and software, but you cannot make every user behave in the same manner even if they use the same device with an identical configuration. In the case of user support, the personality or characteristics of the user (usage pattern) adds to the complexity of the problem. Technology designers have been trying to address these problems by bringing in "ease of use" via GUIs (graphical user interfaces) and in the past decade most of the focus has been accorded to the presentation layer of software in every application. Nonetheless, the support burden has not decreased and contrary to perceptions of vendors (for their self-serving satisfaction), such improvements have only changed the nature of support. There is no doubt, that there has been a significant increase in the numbers of "born digital" and technology savvy users entering the work force, but there is still a significant portion of "digital immigrants" and therefore the need of technical support for non-technical people has maintained its need. But this need may not last for very long. Off late, there has been a rise in the development and maturity of "virtual assistants". And as always, cool tech that is adopted by users at home, always slowly finds its way into the enterprise. All our smart phones have an assistant that can answer questions about the weather, places around us, music travel and traffic, etc. Enterprise IT is no different, the cognitive assistant is on the rise, with several organizations "teaching" the assistant to deal with common queries and to act as the first layer of support at the service desk.

Support in enterprise IT is more focused on resolving incidents or fulling a request, rather than interacting with a customer. It really isn't about who the customer is, everyone now is just an employee number and every incident or request is just an ID with a ticking SLA clock.

Business oriented support and the value of customer in enterprise IT

In the context of user support to external clients, the business reasons are direct and immediate. Good user support leads to customer satisfaction, repeat business, customer retention etc. But, what is the value of a customer in enterprise IT? Do people move jobs because the systems or applications they work on are not as good as another organization? There was a global outbreak of ransomware in the news recently. It was supposedly the largest so far with nearly 200 countries impacted and some very large organizations crippled due to it. A significant number of hospitals and A&E departments in the health service in the UK had to shut down their IT systems. It really was a matter of life and death, as they couldn't access patient records and didn't know if patients were allergic to certain drugs or what medication they were on. Apparently, the vulnerability that was exploited by the criminals was in an out of support operating system. Now, clearly, the IT systems provided to the users of these organizations that were impacted was not the best. Does that mean they would leave and work elsewhere due to this? The equation in enterprise IT is not the same as in a retail environment. The same logic of good support leading to some sort of benefit cannot be applied to enterprise IT. Yes, there is an argument that if you provided good support, a user will be more productive, or at least that users must have the resources required for them to perform their roles. The reality is that in most organizations, IT's budgets have been consistently shrinking and further impacted as the business buy services directly (IT is deemed to be too slow) and the mushrooming of shadow IT. The easiest area to reduce cost is support. Senior or higher value customers continue to get visible support, but for the rest of the work force, it has been moving to "you figure it out". For many years now, there has been a visible thrust of "shift left" where users are discouraged from calling the service desk, but instead first searching through a knowledge base to try and address their issues.

1.2 Service budget shifting

You often hear people complain about cost pressures and expense cuts, especially around budget time. More often than not, it's not that budgets are inadequate. Rather, it's that they are misaligned. History has no shortage of IT projects that spiraled out of control or went massively over budget and still didn't meet the requirement spec or customer expectations. Behind each of these disasters seem to be very familiar trends of unrealistic expectations, the application or systems not working as intended, users not being consulted and poor management. Too many resources are placed into programs designed to make up for poor service design, lack of talent, and a lack of remarkability. Money is too often spent on the latest technology without any concern for what's in the service delivery paradigms. Self-healing is now coming in design but self-serviceability that we see in the business world (airline, banking etc.) is still far away in the corporate or enterprise IT service world

Is Enterprise IT Budget really shrinking?

We have been listening a lot about cost cutting pressure from CIOs. They are given targets to do more with less. On the other hand, the technology spending by enterprises across all industries is growing. So where is that money going? Business leaders in the enterprises are now directly going out and buying technology from niche technology service providers bypassing CIOs. They are willing to spend money for getting the business outcome and those niche service providers are delivering that. Although CIOs have been complaining about "shadow IT" for a long time but in recent past there has been a dramatic reduction in the CIO's share in enterprise technology spending. It is now less than 30%.

What are the options for the CIO? One is short term and tactical. That is outsource and transfer the cost pressure to the outsourcing company. This is actually not solving the problem but transferring a problem. The provider will agree to win the business but eventually the service levels will settle at the price that is being paid. The long term and right strategy is to learn from the trend and become a service provider who delivers on an outcome basis. And then the business will be ready to pay. XaaS service models are suitable for outcome basis delivery and we believe sooner than later, CIO's ought to adopt this.

1.3 Era of digital business

Technology has reached into every aspect of the economy. These could be organizations where technology or related services were their core deliverables, others that were heavily reliant on technology to be able to create and deliver their goods and services or everyone else that used technology to make better decisions. Almost all businesses today have realized that technology plays a pivotal role in their success and in a lot of cases, their survival. Everything from eating out at a restaurant, travelling in a taxi or going on holiday is now entirely influenced by technology and how we find, procure and consume everyday services. Digital businesses blur the line between the physical and digital worlds. The boardroom of a US $50 billion firm was asked who they thought the biggest threat to their business was, a person in the room stated it was *"from a start-up that didn't exist yet"*. The level of almost instant disruption that "digital businesses" have introduced is astonishing.

Businesses have changed, the workforce is younger and have grown up with technology. With the changes in the way we interact and communicate with businesses both as users of their products and services or as suppliers to these businesses, the medium in which support is provided has also substantially changed. Enterprise IT still has a large "human" service desk, but there is a conscious "shift left", which is moving away from a human support desk to online self service, which too has undergone change from self-service based on traditional knowledge articles to crowd sourced support and chat bots to replace human interaction. With most of our interaction now done with mobile screens and internet everywhere, we have well and truly entered the "experience age".

1.3.1 Adaption for the modern world: Customer experience centric

Customer experience is another buzzword, but one that comes with many different interpretations as well as measurement methodologies. Enterprise IT again tends to align a lot of the customer "experience" to satisfaction surveys that its suppliers (or enterprise IT themselves) send out to the user at the resolution of an incident or when a request is fulfilled. Is that sufficient and what customer experience comes down to? Talking of customer satisfaction surveys, I have come across many organizations that ask questions like *"how good was the call with the service desk agent or were they able to resolve your issue? etc."*. The customer experience is the sum of all interactions a customer has with a service provider not merely the support services. The interaction points are during the full lifecycle, from appealing to the customer through marketing (even advertising), engaging during pre-sale and sales cycle, ordering, fulfilling and finally the support. The service provider must work hard and intelligently to make the experience memorable.

Customer experience design starts with customers—who they are and what they want, (and need), and expect. It does not start with an existing product, a new technology, an innovative design, target price point, or bundle of features. It also doesn't assume the channel or delivery method. Customer experience puts the customer at the center and builds out the offering from there. Customer experiences are difficult to produce because they can't be prescribed. No matter how hard you try to script a customer's experience with SOPs, service standards and employee training sessions, a genuine wow experience is almost always a matter of service design.

Most organizations don't bring in radical changes because they are afraid to fail, afraid of the unknown. To them, the unknown is a dangerous place that is too risky and full of pitfalls. Conventional wisdom tells us to avoid danger at all costs and take the safe route.

1.4 Art and science of user experience

Delivering a good user experience is an art because it is an application of human creative skills and also science because it is a systematic and logical body of knowledge. This is what we said in the context of customer satisfaction, and can be repeated for user experience in service management. User experience and customer satisfaction are two different things. The first difference is the party involved. A user is different than a customer though a customer may also be a user. Second, the experience is the impression and feeling on occurrence of the event while the satisfaction is the outcome of the experience.

What constitutes good user experience? How do you even define and measure user experience? Is it the look and feel of a product or the interface of an application? Lets look at the origin of the term, what constitutes user experience and why corporate IT may be focusing their efforts on the wrong thing.

As always, we have a tendency in IT to manipulate terms, make them sound cool, but complex and to suit the latest buzzwords. Unfortunately, many a time, we misinterpret the essence of the intended meaning. I think most people understand and appreciate that the user experience is very important, especially given the choice we have as consumers.

"User Experience" (which cool techies call UX) is a term that was coined by Don Norman, the director of The Design Lab at University of California, San Diego. He created the term in 1993 when he joined Apple as a Fellow and had the job title changed from "User Interface Architect" to "User Experience Architect". As Don Norman explains the rationale behind the term, UX was not intended to refer to just the interface of using a product, but the overall experience that a user has with everything from the buying experience in store, to loading the box in the car (and if that was too big or fit easily), to opening the box and the look/feel of the packaging, to the daunting aspect of assembling and setting up the product, to eventually using it. He says he invented the term because he thought "human interface" and "usability" were too narrow and wanted to cover all aspects of the person's experience with a system, including industrial design, graphics, the interface, the physical interaction, and the manual.

Don Norman is also credited with coining the term "user-centered design (UCD) or user-driven development (UDD)"* which is a framework of processes (not restricted to interfaces or technologies) in which usability goals, user characteristics, environment, tasks and workflow of a product, service or process are given extensive attention at each stage of the design process *(*source: Wikipedia: https://en. wikipedia.org/wiki/User - centered_design).*

So, "User Experience" is about the experience in using the "end to end" service and the experience of that interaction. There isn't a single measure that would provide a score, especially since several of the parameters that form part of the experience are subjective in nature, as well as perception based. Delivering a good user experience is an art because it is a culmination of human creative skills and also science because it is a systematic and logical body of knowledge. It is subjective in nature because it is about individual perception and thought with respect to the system. User experience is dynamic as it is constantly modified over time due to changing circumstances and user behavior. Several aspects can be measured with metrics like: the success rate, error rate, abandonment rate, time to complete an activity in the overall chain, or number of clicks and time taken to request a service or the provisioning or the requesting of support, the availability, etc. There have been 'technical' solutions created to try and measure user experience index, the customer experience index.

1.4.1 User experience by service design vs user experience by service support

Unfortunately, enterprise IT still lags behind when compared to comparable services that users consume outside of the working environment. We all use computers at home and work. There are company provided mobile devices, while others can bring in their own, but use corporate apps on it. We all have a corporate email address as well as a personal email address *(which is likely to be a Gmail id)*, but the experience of using them both is vastly different.

Google CEO Sundar Pichai revealed during an earnings call with investors in January 2016, that their web-based email service had a **billion** users. In May 2017, he revealed at Google's I/O developer conference that their Android operating system crossed 2 billion active devices, so I am fairly confident that the billion users that existed at the start of 2016 grew substantially, although at the time of writing this book I was unable to find any current official stats. Is there a single corporate organization with that scale of end users of email? Anyway, even if you look at a "conservative" billion users, how does the experience of using Gmail compare with your corporate email? When was the last time your Gmail went offline, or you had forgotten your password and had to call the Google service desk? On second thoughts, does Google even have a service desk that you can call? I did find Google forums for each of their products but couldn't find a phone number for their service desk anywhere. On the other hand, most corporate organizations have a fraction of the user base as compared to Gmail, but have large 24x7 service desks. I realize that the service desk supports issues beyond email, but many of the calls received at the desk are related to email and password resets. To compare:

	Gmail	Corporate Email
Number of Users	1 Billion+ users	Varies, but let's say 30,000+ or 0.003% of Gmail user base
Service Desk	None; only online forums	Large 24x7 teams
Availability	Anytime, anywhere, any device – always available	Restricted
User Experience approach	by Service design	by service support

Table 1: Webmail vs Corporate email

Enterprise IT spends a lot of its resources in providing great "support" and then measure the user experience. Extensive discussions and negotiations for more aggressive SLAs for incident resolution are not uncommon when agreeing IT supplier contracts. Many organizations have misinterpreted the essence of 'user experience' and try and build this into the support processes. By then, unfortunately it is too late and a futile exercise. The user's perception of the service and experience has already been negatively impacted.

I accept that comparing services available outside the corporate environment and at work may not be comparing oranges to oranges. Yes, there are budgets to work within, compliance, regulatory and audit requirements in the corporate environment, as well as bureaucratic processes that have to be adhered to, but is that any excuse to not incorporate the "user experience" in the design of the services we provide? And talking of budgets, signing up to Gmail is free.

User experience comes into existence because of user interactions with person or system during the service consumption. A service consumption can be a specific service transaction of a finite and limited duration or perpetual or could be both. For example, obtaining an incident resolution service you may interact with an agent or log in the self-service portal, troubleshoot yourself and fix it yourself. This would be a service transaction. However, using Internet service would be a perpetual service consumption experience.

In a transactional service, the user experience is derived from the channel of interaction and typical non-technical elements are screen appearance including color schemes, GUI and navigation etc. for system interaction and interpersonal qualities such as courtesy, attitude of human at provider end. Both require more artistic approach than the scientific approach because it often does not meet the basic requirements to be considered as science: clearly quantifiable, highly controlled experimental conditions, reproducibility, predictability and testability.

Of course, there are technical elements also such as communication channel quality (voice, network speed etc.) and business processes that can be managed scientifically.

In a transactional service, the experience is attached to one-time transaction and it is transaction specific and does not change with time after the closure of the transaction. Also service warranty (fit for use) and service utility (fit for purpose) criteria are applied to the delivered product.

Perpetual services have a different paradigm of user experience. It is derived from the actual service quality that can be managed and governed scientifically. This is science of user experience. This comes by the design of service. The service warranty (fit for use) and service utility (fit for purpose) are the elements contributing to the user experience in perpetual service consumption and are continually applied to the benefit or the outcome. User experience can dynamically vary with time during the service consumption period. For example, you can be unhappy with Internet service while it is slow and happy again as soon as the performance is restored.

1.4.2 User experience vs customer experience

The terms are often used interchangeably, but 'user experience' is the view from an end users point of view, the ones using the service and the overall experience from that interaction. There are multiple methods to measure the user experience, many of which have their origination in scientific practices, their aims and output are not purely scientific and needs to be tuned to meet the objective, therefore meant as general guidelines, rather than rigid classifications. Traditionally, user surveys have been used in enterprise IT to measure the users experience, but this is a usually flawed approach as it is quite subjective in nature and only really measuring the experience of the support received, rather than the overall user experience. There are multiple methods of measuring user experience and of course with a different focus, namely:

- Attitudinal vs. Behavioral ("what people say "as opposed to "what people do" – and quite often these two can be very different).
- Qualitative vs. Quantitative (qualitative methods are apt for answering questions about why or how to fix an issue, whereas quantitative methods do a much better job answering 'how many' and 'how much' types of questions)
- Context of use (how the product or service is used)

True user's experience is commonly understood as essentially changing due to the constantly changing emotional state as well as the context and difference of use of a service by different users. Aspects of user experience can be measured with metrics like: task success rate, error rate, abandonment rate, time to complete task, or number of clicks to perform a task. In the context of service support, this could be the number of fields to fill and clicks to open a support ticket.

Customer Experience on the other hand, includes all the interactions a person has with a service provider as an organization, this is not limited or specific to a product or service, but the organization as a whole. The distinction being that a 'user' – uses the product, whereas the 'customer' procures the product from an organization. It might be measured in: overall experience, likelihood to continue use, and likelihood to recommend to others. User experience is one of the aspects of customer experience.

I have also come across some clients that are quite keenly implementing the 'net promoter score" (NPS), which in essence is trying to measure the customer experience of interacting with a supplier. More on this later in the book, as I have my apprehensions on the usage of this in a multi supplier environment.

The above distinction is important in a managed services model; as the customer and user could be different.

1.4.3 Can there be a SLA for user experience?

Before answering this question, we need an answer to another question – can we truly measure user experience? I think we have already established the fact that user experience is slightly subjective in nature, as each person's experience could be quite different while consuming the same product or service. Additionally, there is a difference between 'product/service' support and 'user support'.

To understand the characteristics of users, let us look to Hindu philosophy, which argues that there is a continuous and complex interaction that is constant between nature and humans and defines nature as *drishya,* something, which is seen and observed. It consists of two parts, the first being the tangible factors in the external environment, in which a human being lives. The second part, which is what I am referring to are the intangible attributes of a person's personality or character. These attributes are simultaneously present in all humans, although in varying degrees. They also change in quantity at different times of their life. The three personality or character traits are:

Tamogun: It is the tendency in an individual to avoid work, to be contented in whatever is available. They lack ambition. They are lazy in both physical work as well as mental activities. They are not interested in hard work, even if they do get the rewards for it. They tend to have an inclination for evil and are deemed to have negative habits and qualities. Lots of "Tamogun" in a person is not good!

Rajogun: Is a desire for materialistic reward. The individual will do anything and any amount of hard work with a quest for materialistic rewards. The characteristic makes the person feel constantly restless with an insatiable desire for more materialistic things. This creates a competitive spirit and can cause a person to be selfish and less sensitive to other people. Rajogan is not a bad characteristic as it drives ambition and progress in the world, as long as it is channeled in the right direction; but when Rajogun is mixed with Tamogun, it can be a lethal combination and drives bad behavior. You end up with an evil ambitious person!

Satogun: Is the desire for knowledge, wisdom and sense of spirituality. It creates a detached individual who works with devotion and gets a sense of fulfillment with minimal physical needs.

The persona of a person is a combination of the above traits, each in varying degrees of the percentage and shade. In a nutshell, each person is different. On planet earth we already have over 7 billion combinations of Tamogun, Rajogun and Satogun and we shall see this number ever-increasing.

With the latest technology, we can measure the wave length of any color. At my local hardware store, you can take any colored object, they scan it and identify the exact shade. With just 3 basic colors, you can create an infinite number of colors. Unfortunately, this isn't possible with humans. You cannot pin point and identify the traits of a human; besides they keep changing with time and experience. Trying to understand the user experience by a survey or manual methods just does not seem possible. An individual cannot handle the analysis or identification of 7 billion combinations but a computer system using analytics and artificial intelligence (AI) possibly can. Machine-generated support may be more feasible at producing user experience. On the other hand, a computer system cannot offer empathy, which is a critical element of the overall user experience for support services. The emotional connect in support services cannot be produced by a machine.

A significant component of support services are now being pushed towards self-service and empowering the user to help themselves when things do break down. How do you measure the experience in these instances? Is it purely based on how easily they are able to get to the solution and is this directly related to how data is categorized? But the search terms that the user uses will be directly related to how quickly or easily they are able to narrow it down to the right solution. Isn't the user directly therefore impacting the user experience, rather than it being a reflection of the support services from the provider?

Measurement of experience – Index of happiness

"Gross National Happiness" (or GNH) is a philosophy that provides guidance to the government of Bhutan. The term was coined by a British journalist for the Financial Times in 1972. The king of Bhutan at the time, Jigme Singye Wangchuck, stated *"Gross National Happiness is more important that Gross National Product."* It incorporates an index that is used to measure the collective happiness and well-being of a population. Could it not also apply to a corporate enterprise?

GNH is differentiated from "Gross National Product" (GNP) by valuing collective happiness as the goal of governance, by emphasizing harmony with nature and traditional values as expressed in the 9 domains of happiness and 4 pillars of GNH. The four pillars of GNH are:
(i) sustainable and equitable socio-economic development;
(ii) environmental conservation;
(iii) preservation and promotion of culture; and lastly
(iv) good governance.

The nine domains of GNH are psychological well-being, health, time use, education, cultural diversity and resilience, good governance, community vitality, ecological diversity and resilience, and living standards. The domains weigh equally but the indicators within each domain differ by weight. If we are able to measure the product and service and have also figured out how to measure happiness, can the same principles and guidance be used to measure customer experience?

The Dalai Lama had stated that *"not everything can be measured"* in a discussion about western culture. We tend to try and find a scientific explanation of everything and if we are unable to do so, it frustrates us. From the Dalai Lama's point of view – *"we cannot answer every question with a lens of science and technology".*

Every person that uses an IT service interacts with it differently. Each person has different personality traits and emotions, therefore measuring the true experience of each user and the support provided is extremely complex. Everything cannot be measured. We have to be realistic. The investment on the time that it would take, the amount of effort and resources required to truly measure user experience will most likely not lead to any gains. And, if you were to find that the experience of some users was not as good as others, would you really do anything about it? It is of course possible to capture and analyze information on certain aspects that that contribute to the experience that a user has, for example – how quickly a page loads, how quickly a transaction is completed and use this as the basis to make an educated guess at what the experience possible is, but this will still not give you the true measure of every user's experience.

I personally do not think there can be any one single SLA for measuring user experience. As we have seen above, each user interacts with it very differently, so several different aspects of the service can be measured and aggregated to arrive at a figure as they all contribute to the overall experience with some having a higher weightage than others. Besides, the perception of value is directly linked to the cost of the service. As the cost of the service goes up, the perceived value of the service is also reduced. You may say that the experience has nothing to do with the amount of money spent or the cost of the service, but the reality is that when you pay more, you expect a better experience. How do you then factor this into the measurement methodology? If you increase the cost, do you then make each component that you are measuring more aggressive (faster load times, etc.)?

The other issue is that humans are fickle, have a short memory and are willing to forget both the negatives and positives of their experiences. Let's look at an analogy – after standing in the long queue to board the flight, when you get to the boarding desk, if you were to be upgraded, then you forget about the long wait times. It doesn't bother you anymore. You forgive and forget. But when you land, if the airline has lost your bags, then you quickly forget the good experience of being upgraded. We also tend to base a lot of our overall experience of the service with the interaction that happens towards the end of the transaction.

1.4.4 User experience for real business service

User experience (UX) is among the most discussed buzzword these days and there is no doubt about its value and importance. User experience has obtained such a high visibility in the enterprise that we are witnessing the arrival of the CXO (Chief Experience Officer) as a demonstration of commitment and the organizations investment in user experience, as it has quickly become a key differentiator in the 21st century enterprises. So now we should remember to differentiate between CXO and CxO (the generic term for a C level position). A chief experience officer undertakes the responsibility for the overall experience of an organization's products and services by bringing holistic experience design as an intrinsic part of the company's strategy and culture.

All the debates and discussions that I have recently come across are all focused on user experience in the domain of human and computer interaction. Even ISO 9241-210 defines user experience as the ergonomics of human-computer interaction and describes it as "a person's perceptions and responses that result from the use or anticipated use of a product, system or service". So, user experience design tends to focus on the services delivered by computers.

And naturally, the user interface(UI) has become an integral part of user experience as it of course plays a large part in how we experience the system. UI and by default the GUI (Graphical User Interface) form the presentation layer from computer to human. GUI is the "graphical user interface" and UI is just "user interface." GUI is a subset of UI. UI can include non-graphical interfaces such as screen readers or command line interfaces which aren't considered GUI. Following tables explains the different design elements between UX design and UI design and the common collaborative elements between these two.

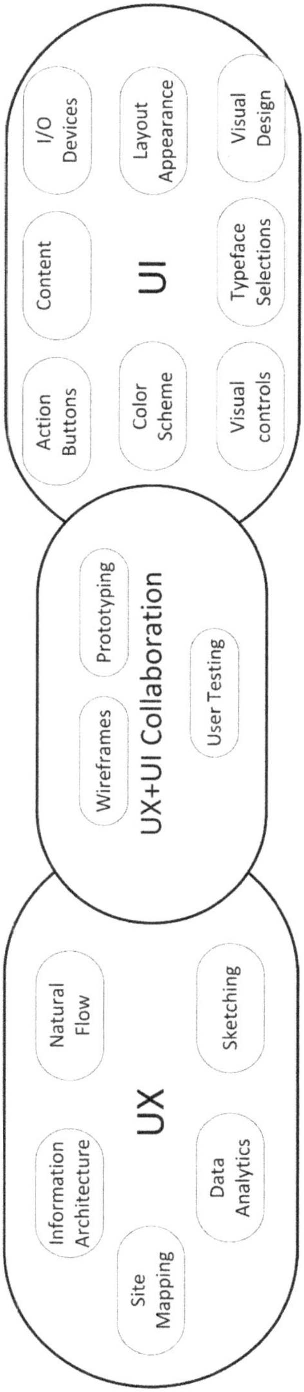

Figure 1: User Experience and Interface elements

While the incorporation of the design elements depicted above would ensure a good user experience for service delivery via an end user device like a computer or mobile and would likely be relevant or sufficient in an enterprise IT context, but this is narrow minded thinking, because the users are "employees" and will probably not quit their job because the experience of using the solutions provided by the employer are not good enough, however, this does not address the broader user experience aspect for a business service where consumers have a choice of products and services and could very easily spend their money elsewhere. The above attributes would be very relevant for digital services, as they are entirely consumed from a device. Enterprise IT should however learn from the airline business, as a significant proportion of their services are not yet digital; the analogy of the airline business has been articulated in figure 2 and 3 below.

User Experience is more than UX and UI design

User experience is a much wider and comprehensive umbrella that includes all aspects of a customer's interaction with the company, its services, and its products and its people beyond services delivered via computers as described by the person that coined the term, so its scope includes business services as well.

That means the business model and business processes of an enterprise have a great impact on the overall user experience. Traditional culture of customer focus and using people, processes and technologies for customer service delivery and service support will continue to contribute to user experience.

Even Gartner divides customer experience efforts into seven types. These are: listen, think, and do (such as collecting feedback); from out to in (changing processes, customer journey mapping, and finding moments of truth); act as one (being consistent across the organization); open up (demonstrating trust, co-creation); get personal (personalizing products, customizing offers); alter attitudes (empowering employees, governance, and policy); and design better (executing brand, executive strategy, and user-experience design). Of course, Gartner calls it CX (Customer Experience) and it is synonymous with user experience.

I was recently at an IBM conference in Vegas, where the President of American Airlines was presenting as part of the keynote speech and talked of the huge efforts that were being put in to improve the overall user experience of their customers and users. So, as an example, I am citing a **Passenger Experience Map** for an airline passenger. It depicts different elements of passenger experience from start to finish in the experience cycle. This can be regarded as **User Experience map for a business service.**

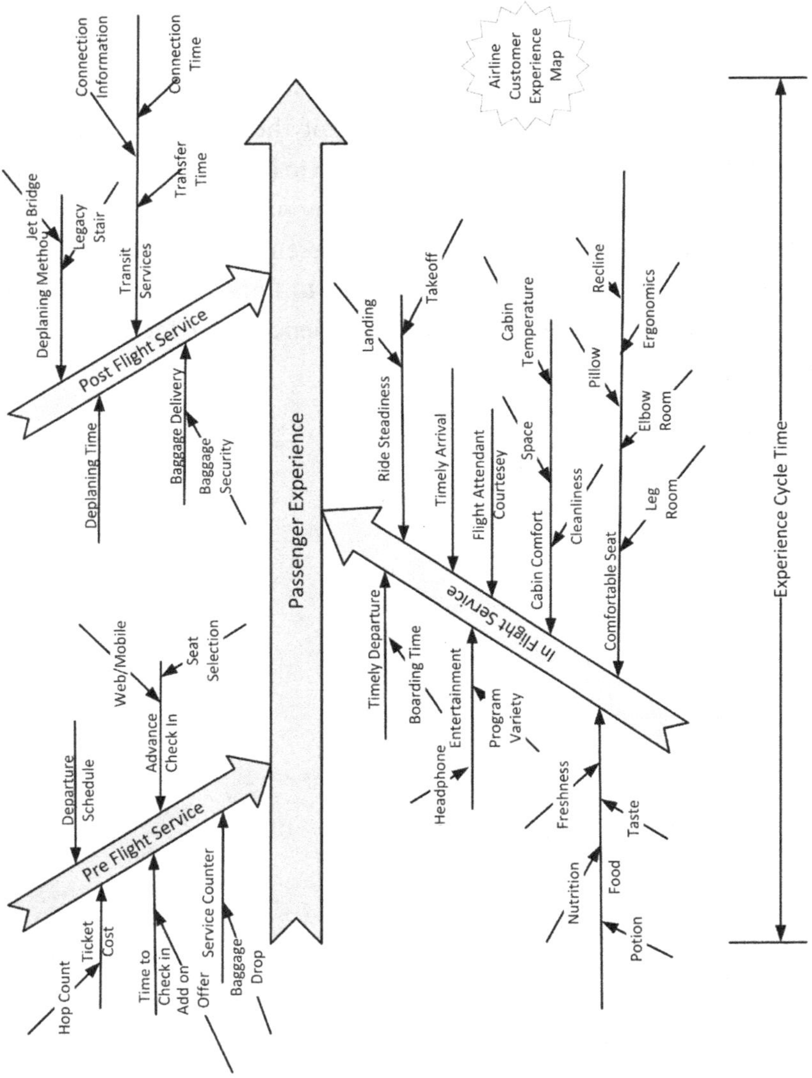

Figure 2: Airline - User Experience components map

You will notice in the UX map, the computer interaction points are the website of the airline, the kiosk at the airport and the entertainment system in flight. All three combined are in reality a very small part of much larger experience map. The very large number of components that join up to create the overall user's experience of flying with any airline start before you have even boarded a plane and continue after you have disembarked. Many of these components can absolutely be further broken down into several smaller chunks, some of which could end up being very complex backend applications, systems and processes (e.g. departure schedules, check-in for passengers) and have interaction and dependency on other third-party systems, compliance requirements; while other aspects may be design related that are done at one time during set up of the service (e.g. leg room). But each of these components all add up to the overall experience. And then, even if all the ducks do fall in a row and everything works seamlessly, there is a possibility that the users experience may be bad for no fault of yours. I was on a flight from London to Los Angeles recently. I wasn't looking forward to being on a plane in cattle class for over 10 hours to start with, however, my expectations were set and everything until boarding the plane had been pretty smooth. When I got to my seat, there was a very large woman sat next to me, who unfortunately just didn't fit within the confines of her seat and I was not only unable to put my arm on the arm rest, but actually had to sit with only half my body on the seat with the other half leaned out into the aisle. The knocks with the passing trolley of drinks added to the discomfort. Now this wasn't the fault of the airline, the service they provided or even the lady sat next to me. The seat space was reasonable and leg room actually better than many of its competitors. But I can tell you, I could not wait to get off the flight and my journey experience was pretty miserable. Now, what I didn't tell you was that I had changed my default allocated seat when I checked in online, as there was someone sat next to me on the seat allocated by the airline system. I got greedy and moved to a seat that had a vacant one next to it. I know I only pay for one seat, so why should I expect an empty seat next to me. But I do this dance of moving seats on the online system before issuing my boarding pass on every journey.

It was probably karma, punishing me for all the greed and wanting more than I deserved or had paid for.

A similar map can be created for IT support services as well. Depicted below are the overall components that will add to the users experience when they request for fulfilment of a service or catalogue item from IT.

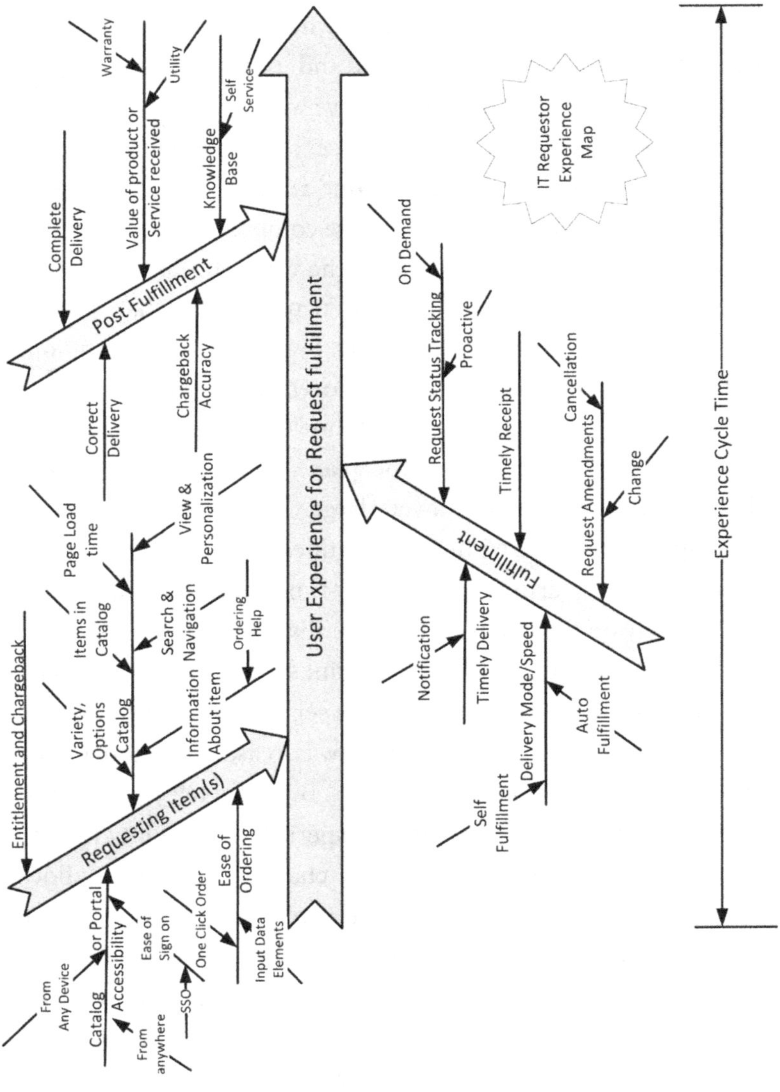

Figure 3: IT Service - User Experience for Request Fulfilment

Another map for the experience of raising an Incident and its resolution is shown below:

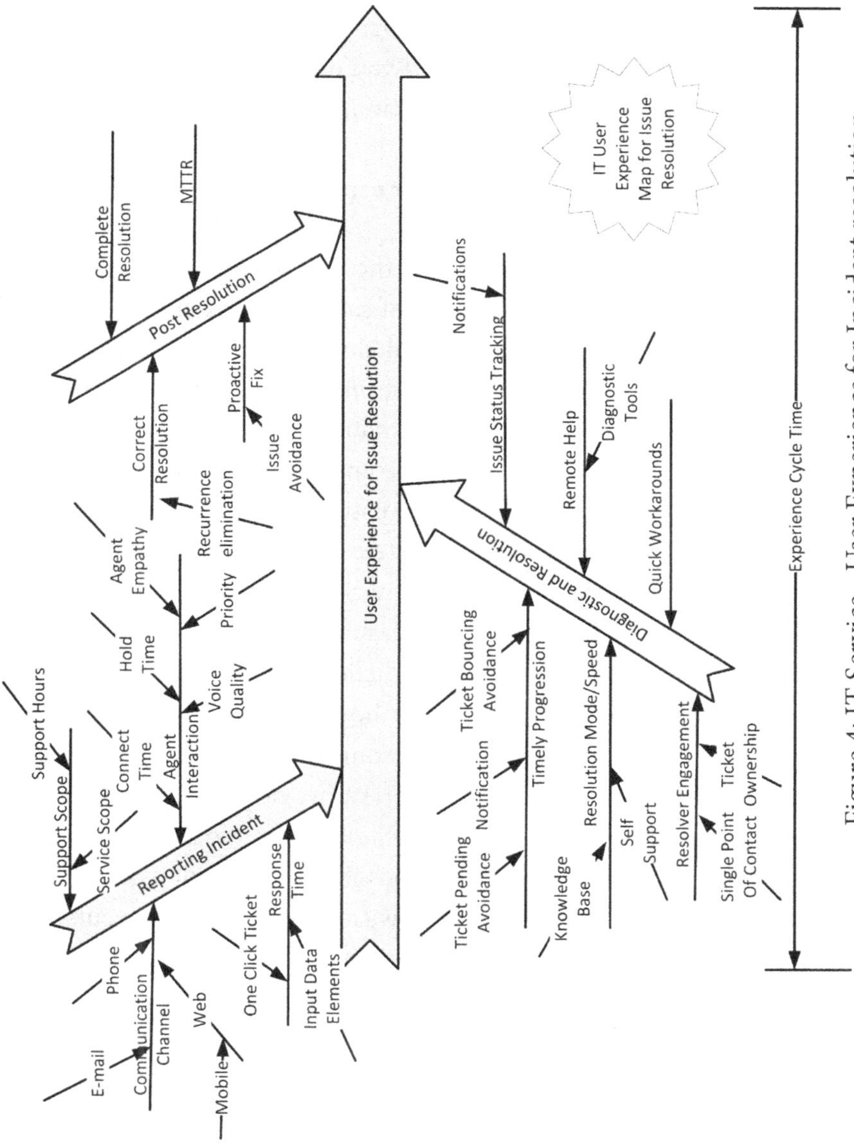

Figure 4: IT Service - User Experience for Incident resolution

The service desk will use this kind of a user experience map for incidents and service requests within enterprise IT to track and manage the end user experience. Most CIO's think that the services they provide are "user centric". In my own experience, I have yet to come across a single organization that has a documented map of each of the services they provide. If you don't have a map for a geography, how will you navigate or optimize your travel route. Similarly, if you don't have a user experience map for your service, how could you optimize it?

1.4.5 How will you measure if the user experience is good?

There are several practices prevalent in the industry to measure the user experience. It is eventually the degree of satisfaction. A simple question with a five-point scale will suffice and do the job, or it could be an indicative question like *"would you use this service and do it all over again?"* But, these are quite subjective in nature and largely depend on the temperament of the user. I haven't come across anything radically innovative or creative in this space to be entirely honest. It is the same old - question/answer, happy and sad faces, etc. The old just gets recycled as something new, but we have a real knack for that in IT!! Customer satisfaction surveys are the closest measure of user experience. These usually try to measure the overall satisfaction, so, was the user satisfied with the service provided. The reality however is that the customers experience of using the service, even something like resolution of an incident is a combination of several criteria as we can see from *Figure 4: IT Service - User Experience for Incident resolution* above; so if a user does say they were not satisfied, it is virtually impossible to pin point what aspect is causing the user to be dissatisfied. So how can you bench mark yourself or analyze which aspects of the service you provide are causing the entire experience to be poor. We could again look at the airline industry; randomly select a cross section of your user base and provide them with an incentive to fill out a more detailed survey that tries to measure all criteria in your experience map and then aggregate and benchmark yourself. This will give you a much better indication of which aspects need to be improved.

The one thing which I think every measurement methodology has in common and agrees on is that the only time to measure user experience is asking the user at the end of the fulfilment of the service, if they had a good or bad experience or enjoyed it. This will usually be quite subjective in nature and is not a scientific measurement as it is a highly personal in nature. One person may have a great experience whilst another may not. It is directly relative to the expectation. The lower the expectation, the higher the likely hood of a better experience. Should we therefore start educating and influencing our users and customers to expect very little from us, because it will probably lead them to be a lot more content with the services enterprise IT provides. Honestly, I had never thought of this until now. Maybe that's the marketing strategy that enterprise IT should adopt!

We have already looked at some examples of how loyalty programs drive a lot behavior in the airline industry and will refer to several others in the next sections. So, there is a fundamental question - does customer satisfaction really matter? Well, I believe that it does not, so long as you have customer loyalty. Loyalty is priceless. If you aim for customer loyalty, customer satisfaction comes along too. People often link customer satisfaction with loyalty but that is not correct. There are ways and means to keep customers loyal, even though they may be dissatisfied, and we see the effective use of these methods by the airline and hotel industry. However, it is also true that a satisfied customer can be made loyal more easily than a dissatisfied one. We cannot completely ignore customer satisfaction. This however will not apply to internal users of an organization.

1.5 Business reality of customer service

Profile of a customer vs the level of a service

Businesses are set up to earn profits, increase market share and revenue for their owners or shareholders. That is a fact with no grey areas. The profit is generated by selling goods and services to the customer. This is done by using the resources of the organization – employees, data, products, systems, etc. When you take the emotion out of it (if there is any), then the plain and simple question is – "does the organization love the customer? Or can the customer love the organization"? The value of a company is derived solely on the share price or potential value of a company. Decisions are made in boardrooms with the sole purpose of maximizing profit. Yes, there are ethical initiatives, sustainability, giving back to the community and other social projects that are undertaken by most large organizations, but the extent to which this can be done is also directly proportional to the profit margins. Good customer service is delivered when it serves the business interest of the organization, but not for any customer. There are multiple models, but if you look at some interesting ones, you will notice that the better service is provided to a selective group of customers, only because they provide more business to the organization. Let's look at loyalty cards and airline benefits. When you have collected enough loyalty points with a particular airline, you move up the coveted next band up colored card. Makes you feel all important, the reality is that you have given the airline enough business to recognize you and reward you for it. You now can start boarding the flight along with the passengers who have paid significantly more than you in the class above. You can use these points to "buy" an upgrade, so you always tend to fly with the same airline, just to be able to collect the points. It isn't that you are loyal to the brand or the organization, you are merely trying to derive the best value, so is the airline. As you move up the loyalty band ladder, the more you fly, your points actually get a multiplier compared to people flying the same distance, only because you are at a higher loyalty card level, basically a higher spender in total. Within enterprise IT, we do have a differentiation with a higher level of service for VIP customers as opposed to the rest of the population.

Generally speaking, people are not willing to wait and want things done instantly. There is an evolutionary instinct to grab the reward as soon as possible and a discomfort in denial. We are hard wired to want immediate and instant gratification, even when it may be unwise. In prehistoric environments, availability of food and other resources was not certain. Like animals around us, humans would survive and grab the smaller reward available to them and skip the larger but delayed reward. The understanding and appreciation may change with age (young adults tend to be more impulsive), but due to us being so used to uncertainty around us, we are conditioned not to trust in a future offer but look to instant gratification. Our sense of time and patience is also altered by our mood. Time always goes painfully slow when you are stuck in a repetitive or boring activity or just having to wait, but time flies by when you are having fun, I guess we have all heard of this. When people are in a state of wanting, time passes slowly. This has created a negative impact on services; people want it now; satisfaction of the customer is driven by expectation and instant gratification sets an incorrect and unrealistic expectation. Even our own internal IT practices have now evolved into doing and delivering things faster.

1.5.1 Digital business world and Enterprise IT world

At a conference, the global head of an application development business made a statement, which has stuck with me ever since. He said, "in a corporate environment, applications are not developed to run, they are designed to meet requirements". What he was saying was that when a development project is taken on, the developers do not really care if the developed application will run when it is lobbed over to the operations team. As long as the application met all the requirements that were stated in the technical, functional and non-functional specifications, then it was job done. This has never been and cannot be the attitude that a digital business adopts. The reason is simple, a retail consumer has a choice. If the service does not their expectations, they can simple use another service. Personal email, personal storage, airlines, news, there are plenty of choices available for users. To avoid a situation where companies start losing their user base, the entire service, interface and experience is designed with the user in mind. And, as we all know, the user base is everything in a digital business. Even if the organization isn't making any profits, as long as the user base keeps growing, the potential future revenue increases and therefore so does the companies valuation. The number of users and the intelligence of their habits is the asset. It isn't the same in a corporate enterprise, applications are not designed to be easy or efficient for the user, they are designed to meet the purpose of the department. The capex/opex application in most organizations is complex, takes ages to process and will demand enough information to ensure you grow old by the time you provide it. This isn't designed with the user in mind. It is the same for expense applications, travel requests, timesheets, etc. So, if the design and purpose of the service or application itself is not the end user, then wont the measure of satisfaction be skewed anyway? Maybe the audience that is being targeted are incorrect, we shouldn't be asking end users of their experience in a corporate environment, we should be asking the department heads if their purpose is being met, no matter what the end user experience is.

Another mistake that is quite common in an IT services provider and client scenario is, the sycophancy or yes-man approach, it does not contribute to good customer service. Trying to please the customer by always saying yes can quickly lead to disastrous consequences. I have seen several situations where the client was asking for and doing the wrong thing and the suppliers agree to do it anyway, including asking for services at an unreasonable cost. This may lead to short term gain but could also hurt the reputation of the supplier in the long run. When discussing current pain areas when negotiating a new contract, a customer stated that their existing supplier provided no thought leadership, never said no, provided services at a low cost and therefore cut corners, and if the client asked them to jump off a bridge, they wouldn't stop to think. There is a difference between making a customer happy and pleasing a customer! There are lots of differences in the way that a digital business or even business will operate when designing and building services for consumers, compared to how they operate when delivering services to their internal users, i.e. enterprise IT. This book is written largely in the context of enterprise IT.

The intention of this book is not to provide you with a list of SLAs that you should adopt with your suppliers. The reality is that if you are using cloud services (or "as a service" delivery models), then you do not have the option of creating your own SLAs anyway. Depending on the level of service you buy, the SLAs that will be applicable will differ. And if you are procuring legacy, or traditional IT services, where everything is custom built based on your requirements, then the SLAs you agree and negotiate will depend entirely on your business needs, the cost of the service, the architecture of the environment, etc. Sadly, we have come across several examples, where advisors and consultancies are engaged to help clients. Rather than guide and coach the client on how to make the right decisions, they coach them on what decisions to make. We did not want to adopt this fundamentally flawed approach and have therefore not provided a list of SLAs.

2 SLA Indoctrination

2.1 What is a SLA?

A SLA is a formal, written and signed ***agreement*** between a service provider and a client. It lists and describes the services to be provided, by whom, at what frequency, and to what standard. It also lists the metrics by which that service is measured and the remedies or penalties, if any, should the agreed upon service levels not be achieved. Once compiled and agreed, the SLA forms the sole terms of reference against which the effectiveness or failure of the service provider is measured.

The word 'agreement' has a share of implied meaning. Synonyms are contract, commitment, arrangement, understanding and covenant. A legally binding agreement is usually a contract, but an SLA can also be made as a memorandum of understanding (MoU) that is not legally enforceable.

In most outsourcing deals, SLAs form part of the contract and are legally binding.

A SLO (Service Level Objective) is another term used in lieu for a SLA when the service provider is not willing or unable to accept the contractual obligation or penalties for when the SLA is not achieved, but accepts and agrees to the target to provide the service level in good faith. It is also quite common in traditional IT outsourcing deals, to start the engagement with an "SLO" for a few months, before the "SLAs" kick in. This is usually done to allow the incoming service provider to get a handle on the environment and increase their knowledge of the business applications, which in all likelihood will be a pre-requisite for them achieving the SLAs. In the "as a service" (or XaaS, where "X" could stand for anything or everything) delivery model, this is less common. More on that later.

2.1.1 What do SLAs do?

SLAs are generally perceived as a legal tool to achieve the business goals of obtaining the required service level. This is indeed very unfortunate, because all the focus is shifted in writing a strong contract to protect the client's interests and to create a stick that the service provider can be beaten up with, rather than writing a good SLA that actually steers towards providing a good service.

Listed below are six very important purposes or criteria of an SLA, none of which would traditionally form part of a contact, whose sole purpose is that of creating a legally binding document.

(i) Define the product and service to be provided

What "thing" a customer will receive is central to all SLAs. If a service provider cannot define what they are delivering, then they do not know what they are delivering. The ability to clearly articulate and define the deliverable is the first step towards building the capability to meet the SLAs. It is very important and critical to define whether a service provider's definition of a service is the execution of a task or delivery of an output or the delivery of an outcome. Definition of the deliverable also help to define the measurements around it. Execution of tasks is a viable service definition and a rudimentary service as well. The next level is the definition of output and a highly mature SLA can define the outcome in the service definition. In several cases, especially in managed IT service outsourcing, what the service provider will do becomes the definition of the service, but the measurements are defined around the outcome. This is fundamentally incorrect and sets everybody up for failure.

(ii) Establish the *manner* in which the product and service will be provided

It is not only what is delivered, but the way they are delivered that are equally important. Everyone looks for good manners in a person; similarly, a customer should also look for good manners in the service – the way a customer will receive the service. In the context of an SLA, the manners are the direct and indirect methods of service delivery and support that are listed in the definition of the services. Some of the methods that have a direct impact on the service quality and/or customer interactions, should be included but not backend methods utilized by the providers, which has no direct bearing on the service quality and SLA or customer interaction. For example, in support services, remote support or local support, e-mail support or phone support etc. establish the manner in which the support services will be provided. Needless to say, courteous style of the service provider's support resource interacting with the user could also be thought as a part of the manner but that is implied, and it is assumed that everyone will follow good business ethics and behavior. However, the language spoken during the interaction is a vital part of service support and delivery. So, the SLA should mention at least the top-level methods that will be used to provide the service. It is like just saying, "*we will provide a taxi service*" is not good enough; you need to be clear and specify if it is a saloon car, Mercedes, minibus, has air conditioning, boot space for how many full-size suitcases, etc.

(iii) Establish the quality standard to be achieved

Every service listed in the SLA definition section must have explicit quality parameters. In IT outsourcing, especially in telecommunication and infrastructure services, the QoS (Quality of Service) is a well-known acronym and provides industry accepted quality parameters. However, in a managed service model, there is a lot of complexity as it involves people in addition to the technology used. Managed service SLAs are more than the SLAs of technical systems defined in isolation.

Enterprise IT outsourcing has been done using a managed service model for more than 15 years now and along the way, we have learned to define the quality parameters of managed services. In fact, we believe that those are over defined. We only want to emphasize that it is essential to establish the parameters that are sensible and pragmatic.

(iv) Establish metrics and measurement criteria

I think everyone knows the famous saying – *"if you cannot measure it, you cannot manage it"*. The first three steps listed above would not be of much value if you could not establish the measurement criteria against the quality parameter for each service. It is better to strike out the service from the scope of the SLA document if you cannot measure the service level itself. As said earlier, the technical QoS and for technology centric services, it is usually easily defined and as is the system instrumentation for that, therefore relatively easier to measure that. The problem comes in the upper layer, i.e., the non-technical service that runs on top of the technology. For example the services at the layer of business processes and services delivered with the components of human actions.

The SLA around the application and business process layer is usually the point of instrumentation deficiency; either the instrumentation is not available or not adequate to measure. If those parameters are really critical for the business, then they may consider investing in developing the instrumentation and measurement system. Alternatively, you could always fall back on an alternate workaround method. For example application or business process availability can be measured by the incidents reporting time and the mean time to resolve (MTTR) data. This is not an accurate measurement but a workaround to give you some idea about the down time. If the measurement is for parameters of the service that has human action components, then this involves the design of correct processes and procedures that will capture the data-points in the service management system.

(v) Establish reporting criteria

Measurement will likely be spread across multiple data sources and multiple measurement systems. Historically report producing and publishing was quite elaborate and a cumbersome, manually intensive task. Now, technology is advanced enough to make an affordable dashboard that can consolidate data from multiple sources without them having to follow a common, predefined structure, and publish reports in a personalized form. The consumers of reports will also be across multiple groups with varied interest and focus areas; the dashboard could be easily configured for each individual's preferences.

(vi) Negotiate and determine cost of delivery

Having reached this stage, you should by now have a handle on all the aspects of the services in SLA scope. This will enable you to determine and negotiate the cost for the services. Sometimes, you may go backward to redefine the quality parameters of a service in SLA in order to meet the cost target. SLAs have a direct bearing on the cost of delivery, as it may require additional technology (driving up cost of implementation, licenses, software maintenance, upgrades, etc.) and/or additional resources to deliver at the agreed service levels. Cost and pricing related information form an integral part of all SLAs, but the best practice is to keep it as an annexure in the contract. SLAs are widely circulated among many stakeholders in the organization but costs are deemed to be confidential or restricted information. By keeping it separate, it becomes easy to share an unrestricted SLA document.

2.1.2 Important Points in a SLA

While more details will be covered in the subsequent sections, listed below are the basic and essential points that need to be covered in SLAs.

(i) Stakeholders

While there would be a set of common services such as e-mail or personal storage that would be used across all the users in an enterprise, there could likely be department or function focused services as well. Diversified users and diversified services will usually be included in one SLA. So it is important to include the right stakeholders - names of the departments or groups in relationship with representative's names in the SLA document.

(ii) Service Description

Description of the service to be provided should be clearly articulated in a user understandable language, not in the providers' operation form. What the service will provide to the user, what will make it fit for use and fit for purpose should be clearly stated in the description.

(iii) Business drivers and priorities

SLA is a business document after all and if lower service levels can serve the purpose then why spend money on higher service levels? I have always seen this principal in the business world but in enterprise IT, I have observed that many SLAs are set at a higher level without any business justifications (remember they drive up costs too!).

(iv) RACI

Roles and responsibilities of all the parties involved must appear in the form of a RACI chart. This includes service receiver (users) as well and that is often missed. RACI is a very good format provided it is understood well. One basic principle of RACI that is misunderstood is about responsibility and accountability. I have often seen multiple parties appear in the accountability column, I believe this is a faulty concept. Joint accountability is a weak proposition. You ought to have one neck on the line.

(v) Service delivery methods

Service delivery process at the top level including the media and method of delivery will form an important part of the SLA document. Typical examples include contact method, language, geography of task execution, technology used etc.

(vi) Performance measures

Of course, what are the metrics and indicators that the SLA is being achieved is an integral part of all SLA document.

2.1.3 Benefits of SLA

A well-written SLA delivers several benefits. A few of them are worth mentioning.

(i) SLAs establish *two-way* accounting for service

Strange as it sounds, but the customer should also know how to get a good service, it is not the sole responsibility of the service provider. The RACI will clearly call out what role the customer has to play, in several other instances, it is also implied.

Everyone uses a smartphone today, some get more value out of it than others. If you use it for less than what it can give, you do not get the full benefit, for example, if you only use a smartphone as a phone, or only use email and a browser, you do not get the full value, even though it can run numerous other apps, but it will meet your needs.

Additionally, within a corporate IT environment, if a user complains about a business application not working and the service desk asks for a screenshot of the error, additional information and puts the ticket into a pending state (stopped the SLA clock), then it will take longer to resolve your issue. There is two-way accountability to provide information and participate; if the user doesn't meet their obligation, the end service and user experience will likely be poor. It is also common to hear users say *"you are the expert, you figure it out"*. Do you ever go to the doctor and say *"I am unwell, but you figure it out as you are the expert"*. Naïve users will always get poorer service than expert users. It is also not just the experience of the end user that could be impacted, but may also affect the performance of the service provider – the unilateral attitude of one party could cause the SLA to breach. As controversial as it sounds, a customer usually gets the service they deserve.

(ii) Create levels of service that are negotiated and standardized

The SLA establishes a clear level of expectation of the service that they will receive and at what cost. The variables are known, which could either drive up the cost of the service or the performance. It also creates a baseline which can be built upon when increasing the level of service or setting stretched targets.

(iii) Document service level in writing

When things are documented, there can be no ambiguity or things getting lost in translation. It is of course vital not to just document the SLA, but exactly how it will be measured, what will be used as the source of data and each parties' role. A well-documented service level will provide a balance between being thorough and clear on one side, while on the other side, not being overly tedious on the service provider.

(iv) Clearly defined criteria for service evaluation

The criteria for evaluating the level of service will be absolutely clear to both parties. They set the tone for the relationship between the parties and will govern if and when things break down. It should also assist with looking at the right areas to drive improvement.

(v) Provides basis for improving service level

If the expectation, measurement methodology and source of information is clear, driving up service levels to improve the service or even analyzing and jointly working to resolve situations when the agreed service levels are not achieved should be a lot easier.

(vi) Standardizes methods for communicating service expectations
If the SLA is documented, set clear criteria, then communicating and setting the expectations of users should be a lot easier. I have come across several customers, where users have been complaining of a poor service; however on looking at the performance reports of the suppliers, they were all being achieved. The perceived service was poor, because the expectations of the user had never been set, no matter how good a service the provider delivered, the user was always disappointed. Now that I think of it, this also seems to be case with my wife! No matter how quickly I get things fixed in the house, she always seems to think I take too long and never get things done when she asks - maybe an SLA is in order!

2.1.4 Calamity of SLA

SLAs drive behavior

Not sure if you have heard about "herding cats"; this is a very common issue with IT folks. If you had to get a dog from point A to B, then a collar and lead will usually get the pooch to follow you. Try doing that with a cat. Forget about getting to point B, you will be lucky if your feline friend doesn't claw your hands while at the first stage of getting the collar on! To get a cat to point B, you have to put treats at strategic points to get the cat to follow the path you choose and get to your desired destination. IT folks are like cats. IT resolver groups will do work with the sole consideration of attaining the agreed metrics, no more and no less. This is because they believe that their performance is measured solely on achievement of the numbers. This is not the right way in a process or service paradigm. However, in the real world, metrics will drive the behavior in the organization. What gets measured, is what gets done; so, metrics should reflect a complete understanding of goals and objectives. If you are measuring how many incidents a support person resolves, you can expect a sudden increase in the ticket volume—tickets will be created only to get resolved and attain better metrics. Or tickets will be quickly resolved to reach a volume target, with no consideration on the quality of resolution provided. For example, I heard about Continental Airlines' measurements to achieve fuel efficiency. They measured pilots for fuel-efficiency targets. Pilots found a variety of ways. One of the easiest was to reduce the cabin temperature. You make passengers uncomfortable but save fuel!

Meeting SLAs vs meeting the intent with spirit of the SLA

Despite all the explanations, clarifications and definitions, there are some aspects of the service that will still remain open to interpretation and individual understanding. At this point the spirit or the intent of the SLA should become the guiding principal. When the metrics and targets drive the behavior and actions, the spirit to focus on the intent of the SLA almost always disappears into the background. An incorrect interpretation of the SLA leads to bad service.

A typical example is *"First call resolution"* (FCR) at the service desk. The "intention" is for the Service Desk to not become a "catch and dispatch" *(or log and flog)* function, where they do not have enough knowledge and skills to resolve a significant number of calls at the desk. If there are no other SLAs to drive the behavior, this will lead to the service desk agent keeping the user on the phone for a long time, even if they know it will take longer or try and figure things out while the user is on the phone. This will lead to the SLA numbers being met, but meeting the intent of the SLA, which was to provide a better service by increasing the knowledge of the desk, handing over the authority to the desk to perform additional tasks being completely defeated. Another one is *"speed to answer"*, a service desk agent will answer the call quickly even if they are on another line and likely put the user on hold while they finish their first call off. If the user drops off in frustration, they would have breached no SLA, as they answered the call within the agreed time and since they never got to logging the ticket, no FCR SLA applies anyway. If the intent isn't understood, just these two SLAs can ruin the experience at any service desk, while the service provider will continue to meet their targets!

Focus on evidence of doing right vs focus on actually doing it right

SLAs always bring in an element of bureaucracy in the organization. It establishes a system of governance in which most of the important decisions are made by influential managers rather than by service users. If something goes wrong or targets are missed, then service providers have to prove that they did the all the right things and produce evidence to support their position. The importance of evidence and maintaining an audit trail is usually learned after encountering a few issues and this approach of *"gathering evidence just in case"*, is adopted. The focus on doing it right diminishes, as the focus shifts to doing the right things – in order to protect yourself rather than provide a good service.

2.1.5 Where do SLAs work?

Most people perceive an SLA as a huge monolithic document, that is created to serve the purpose of bureaucracy. Yes, it does, but, bureaucracy has its benefits and is inevitable in any big organization.

SLAs works well where bureaucracy works

SLA is an agreement after all and a document of responsibility and accountability. Whenever you need to monitor the responsibility and accountability, monitoring and reporting needs to be transparent and open with clear norms and rules. This will introduce a system of processes and authorities that form the elements of bureaucracy. In our earlier publication *"Process Excellence for IT Operations"* we had elaborated on ways of how to avoid inefficiency and yet maintain the positive aspects of bureaucracy. However, it is worth repeating a small portion of that here again:

Bureaucratic Approach	Process Approach
Strict adherence to rules without consideration of purpose	Purpose driven performance of a defined set of activities
Iron cage of control to pin down accountability	Flexible control within defined boundaries
No empowerment	Empowerment within boundaries
Empowerment within boundaries	Requires judgment
Noncompliance will lead to disciplinary action.	Noncompliance will have an impact on purpose/quality.
Focus is to show that things were done right.	Focus is to do the right things.

Table 2: Bureaucratic vs Process Approach

SLAs work in a predictable environment

SLAs work in an environment where the amount of work is predictable, and the type of work is similar. A SLA is primarily written in advance for the scenarios and the services that are predetermined and predictable. If there are seasonal variations in the service demand, those are also known in advance and incorporated in the service delivery methods to accommodate them. Unpredictable or diversified work will have a direct impact on the SLA or ability to execute and deliver. Exception clauses in the SLA usually address these. Also, the SLAs are totally different in disaster scenarios.

Size of the organization does matter

SLAs work in large organization, which are committed to tight controls. Large organizations are designed to work with standard systems, processes, governance and the bureaucratic approach that is a necessary component for SLAs to work.

SLAs require resources

It is not just a matter of resources to deliver and support the services, but resources are required to manage and govern the performance of SLAs as well. SLAs work where there are sufficient resource and management time to manage SLAs and service providers

SLAs work where there is authority to design and represent them

Stakeholders of SLAs are diversified groups across the enterprise and they must be represented with adequate authority in the entire process from developing the SLA to governing the achievement of SLAs.

2.1.6 Need of SLA for insourced services

SLA in its perceived form is not mandatory need to deliver services, but what is necessary is to meet the purpose and the intent of the SLA. You could write a proper SLA that could be short and yet meet the purpose of both the parties - service provider and customer. In a small organization a simple service statement could quite easily replace a SLA.

Another important aspect of a SLA is that it provides definite written goals. We cannot do things that we would like to do and are capable of, unless we have a written definite goal. If a simple service statement can serve that purpose, then why increase the complexity?

The purpose of a SLA can be adequately achieved for insourced services with an agreed SLO and documented targets. As stated earlier, SLO (Service Level Objective) is another term used in lieu for SLA when the service provider is not willing to accept the contractual obligation for the SLA but accepts the target to provide the service level in good faith.

Having targets for internal teams is especially important in a multi-supplier environment. The reason is that services provided by external providers and internal teams usually have a dependency on each other to deliver an end to end service. If the service providers meet their obligations, but the internal teams drag their feet, the perception of the overall service by end users will be poor. Additionally, CIO's of most large IT organizations have a vision and ambition for their IT departments evolving to be an IT broker, where all services are procured externally, as a service, aggregated and provided as one end to end service to their users. There is constant pressure to do more, better, for less. Unless you have an understanding of internal costs and also how the services they provide compare to services available in the market, there is a risk that you will drive the business to go directly and buy services externally. After all, it is them who control the purse!

2.2 ITIL concepts and beyond

The ITIL concepts of *Operational Level Agreements* (OLA) and *Underpinning Contracts* (UC) continue to still exist and are applicable, as legacy IT still remains in almost every large organization. However, this concept will slowly dwindle and will be replaced by "SLAs in XaaS Model". There are multiple providers in the supply chain, each one playing a specific role. We have looked at this in further detail in section *"2.2.3.1 - Service Chain entity in XaaS model"*. In the XaaS world, you will focus only on the SLA with the last provider who provides it to the end user. All the supply chain roles behind the last provider are invisible to the user and of no relevance to the end user. The concepts of UC, OLA will completely vanish.

ITIL has provided guidance in the Service Level Management process to implement the service delivery chain concept from a user's and customer's perspective. ITIL has established the relation between Service Level Agreement (SLA), Operation Level Agreement (OLA) and Underpinning Contracts (UC); however the guidance on implementation is virtually missing. In most cases SLAs and UCs are adequately defined and constructed, but OLAs do not exist or are very adhoc (read chaotic). I have provided my own experience and opinion on OLA's further below.

ITIL defines OLA as follows:

An OLA is an agreement between the IT Service Provider and another part of the same organization. An OLA supports the IT service Provider's delivery of IT services to customers. The OLA defines the goods or services to be provided and the responsibilities of both parties.

An Operational Level Agreement is very similar to a SLA but is non-contractual in nature, describes the method of collaboration, goals to be achieved, and measurements of different groups for the common purpose of achieving the SLA targets. In simple terms, it is a document that captures how the groups will work together and how quickly they will respond when they receive a request for support. Therefore, the OLA establishes the RACI among the functional groups in IT organization.

My personal experience with OLA's haven't been promising. I will discuss this in the subsequent sections.

Simplistic view of SLA, OLA and UC

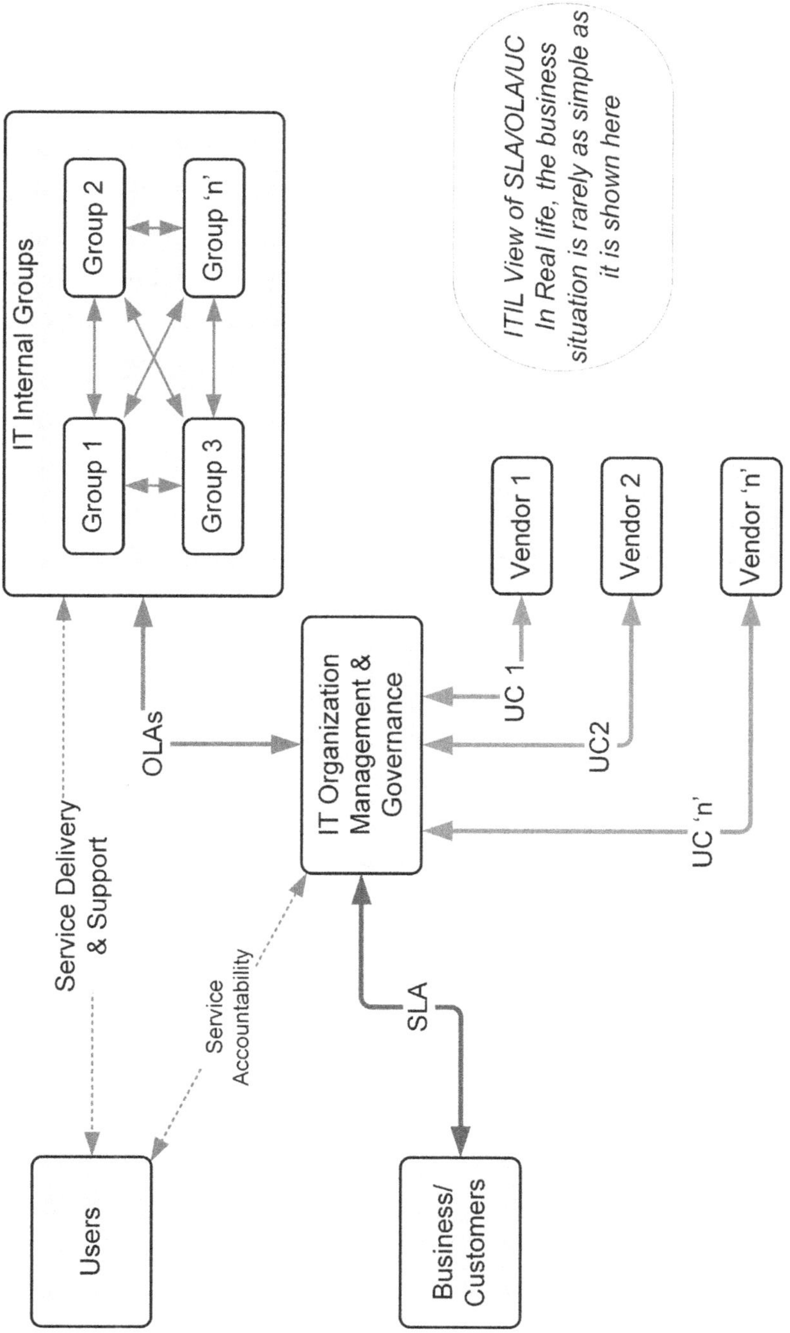

Figure 5: ITIL View of SLA, OLA and UC

There is a slight difference in the ITIL terminology and in a real-life scenario as depicted in the diagram above.

1. ITIL OLA is an SLA
2. UC is service contract
3. ITIL SLA is nonexistent

The diagram below depicts a typical situation with SLA, OLA and UC in Gen 1 outsourcing with a single vendor. You will quickly notice how the complexity increases and how different it is to a simple "theoretical" view shown above.

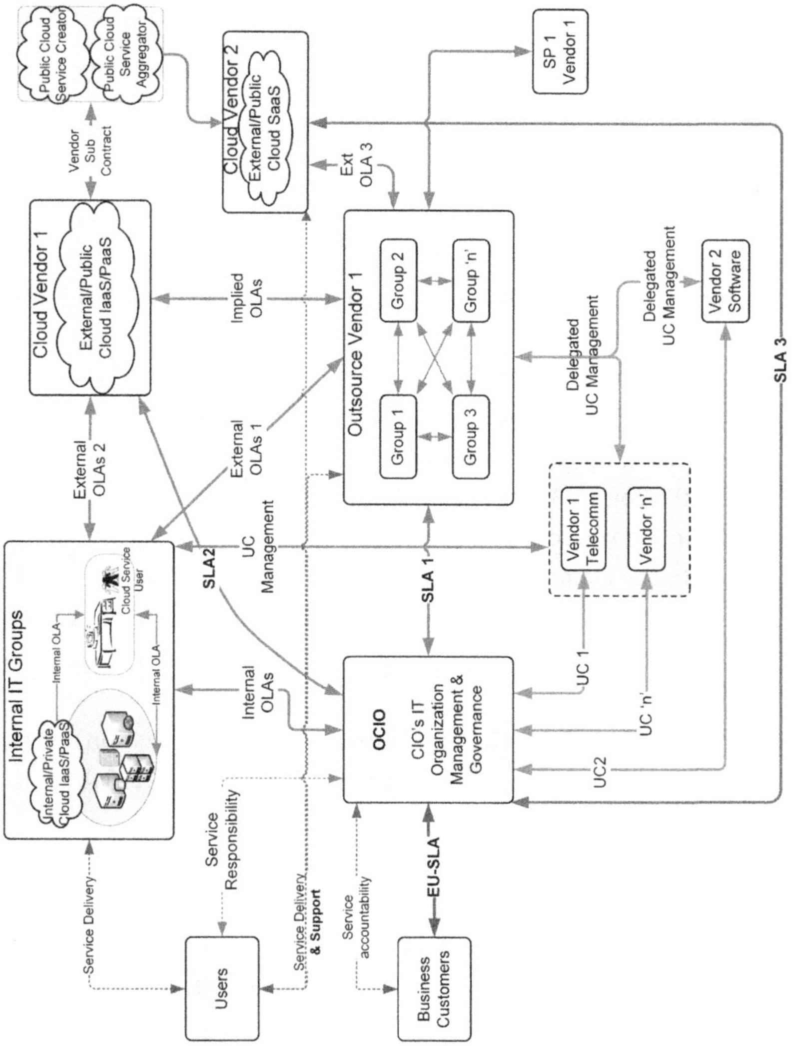

Figure 6: SLA, OLA and UC in Single Vendor outsourcing

You will by now realize, that things are not as simple as depicted in a theoretical ITIL book. It is not just contracted SLAs, but you quickly get into situations where there is an implied responsibility, delegated responsibility and the requirement to manage vendor contracts on behalf of the client. In the above diagram:

1. **Internal OLA** is the OLA among the towers retained by the IT organization.
2. **External OLA** is the OLA between groups of the retained IT organization and outsourced vendor.
3. **Delegated UC Management** is management of the underpinning contract (UC) signed between the IT organization and the third parties. This means the outsourced vendor will use the service provided by the third-party vendors and deliver the SLA to the IT organization. This will also allow the outsourced vendor to enforce the contractual terms on behalf of the IT organization.
   The outsourced vendor may also have its own vendors which will not be visible to the client's IT organization. The outsourced vendor may subcontract one or more parts of the service to its own vendor. However, the contractual obligations will remain with outsourced vendor.
4. The **EU (end user) SLA** is the SLA between the IT organization and the customer. This is usually non-contractual as it is internal to the business.
5. **SLA:** SLA in the co sourcing model will usually refer to the contractual SLA between IT organization and the outsourcing vendor.
6. The IT organization will still be accountable for the services to customers and end-user although, the outsourced vendor will assume the responsibility.

2.2.1 SLA in a Multi-supplier environment

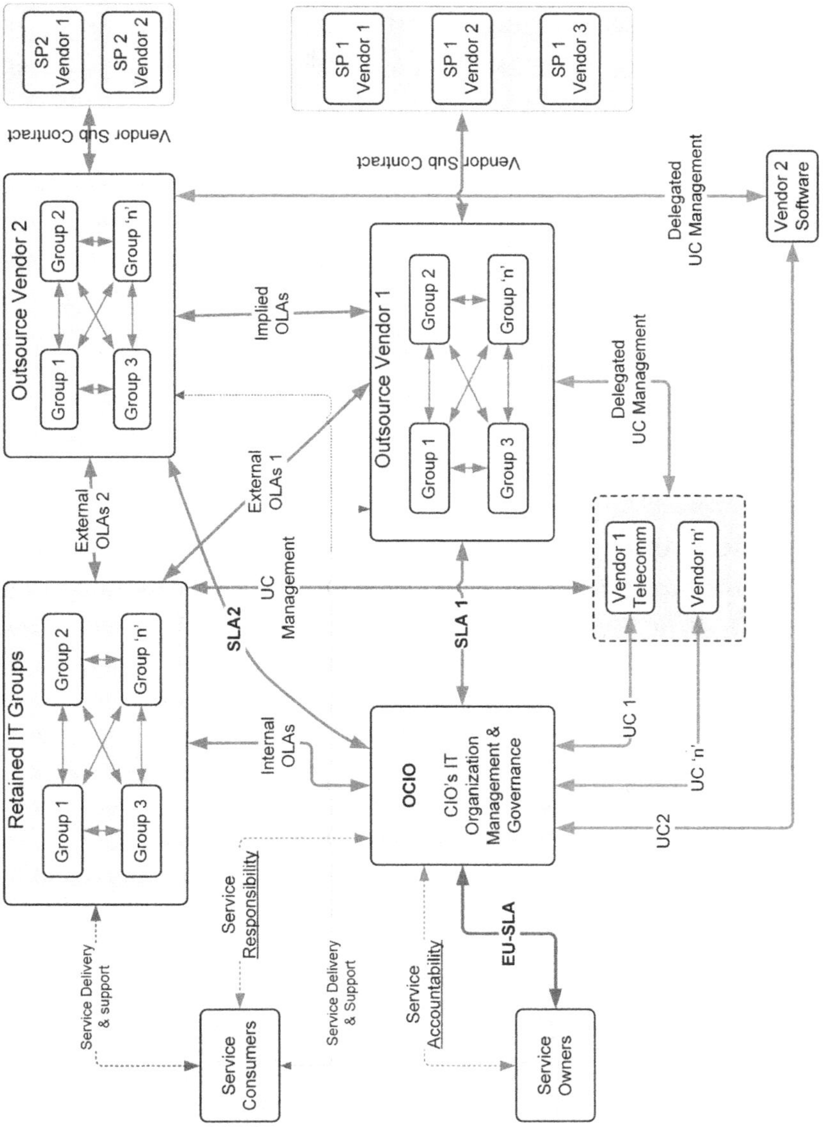

Figure 7: SLA, OLA and UC in multivendor outsourcing

The matrix gets even from complex in a multi supplier environment. There is complex dependency between suppliers. It is also very common to find that the SLAs that clients agree with each supplier are entirely different, which each working to vastly diverse goalposts. Instead of focusing on making things simpler, we end up complicating it even further.

Service Integration & Management (SIAM) is the management methodology that is usually adopted in a multi-vendor sourcing approach, which necessitates the need for an overarching service management function that is responsible for integrating the services provided into a set of end-to-end service outcomes. The SIAM function is also responsible for governance, coordination, auditing, process alignment between the suppliers and ensuring the suppliers work together as one cohesive unit.

My experience of this area is that it is fraught with pitfalls and risk of seriously over-complicating what is required. This isn't made any easier due to the client having vastly different SLAs with each supplier. The expectation from the client however, is that the SIAM function will manage it all, simplify it, define even more end to end SLAs that the suppliers will all sign up to.

A well-regarded advisor, whose opinion most clients will refer to as the gospel truth, puts a lot of emphasis on OLAs being the core ingredient in a multi supplier recipe. I have a very different opinion of what actually happens in real life. In all of time of being involved with service management deployments, I have not come across many organizations that have had formal OLAs documented. I could possibly count them on one hand. My own personal experience has been that an OLA, although a non-contractual document, very quickly leads to a commercial and legal discussion. Let me elaborate and explain what I mean. When one IT service provider, discusses an OLA with another supplier in the ecosystem, they will usually try and negotiate a response time that enables them to meet their agreed SLA. I had a client, who had agreed a 4-hour resolution time with their infrastructure provider for all priority 2 incidents, but an 8-hour SLA with the applications provider, for the same priority. When the infrastructure provider required the applications provider to respond in under 2 hours, the application provider stated that they weren't sized to respond so quickly. If the client needed this, then there would be a commercial impact and require a contract change. As you can imagine, every supplier started including statements to cover themselves and account for every eventuality, it quickly led to becoming a huge document, with lots of legal language, etc. A document that couldn't be widely circulated, certainly not to the operations team, who were the one who have to execute. So as easy as it sounds, depending on who the parties to an OLA are, they are not very easy to agree or execute. We have come up with several other methods of achieving the same objective or an OLA. I would even go as far as questioning the real-world applicability of OLA's!

I will provide some overview of some of the weird and wonderful SLAs I have come across, hopefully we can understand and come to a logical conclusion of if we really need so many SLAs and OLAs and UCs.

2.2.1.1 Measuring End to End and supplier SLA achievements

In spite of all of the challenges of operating in a multi supplier environment, the reality is that it isn't going to go away. Multi Sourcing is the norm in most large enterprises today. It is quite common to find even single technical towers continuing to be split into multiple suppliers due to the global landscape; for example, end user support services which require close physical proximity to the user and it is quite possible that a single supplier may not be set up in every country that a client may be operating in. Customers want to source and deal directly with suppliers best positioned to provide the service and help them propel their business, rather than a single prime contractor. The trend has also been for contract durations to be much shorter than they used be 10 or 15 years ago, which inadvertently creates a need for robust capability to be able to onboard new suppliers or off board existing suppliers seamlessly and without any impact to end users and of course measure their performance as they deliver services. Not just their own individual performance, but the end to end performance as well. Every Supplier is only working to fulfil their own contracted scope of services, within their agreed SLA. This may be an application that provides some capability or functionality or hardware services, but more than likely will not constitute an end to end service, which therefore creates a need to measure the end to end performance after the discrete components have been aggregated across a multitude of suppliers.

Integrating suppliers can be done in several different ways. The way their performance is measured will still fundamentally stay the same, but the way it is done will differ. The first thing that likely be different is where and how they are integrated. "e-bonding" is a common term used when the suppliers and the clients service management tools are integrated using methods like web services or API integration. This provides the updates and information in real-time, but can be cumbersome to put in place, takes time and requires ongoing maintenance effort. Although processes like incident, change, request management are commonly integrated using these methods, other processes are a lot rarer to do, so you end up in a mixed mode. Some alternate methods used are email integration, where the system sends the update via an email, which the receiving system uses to update records, as well as a manual swivel chair method, which is nothing but a human keying in information in multiple tools. Some of the factors that you will refer to before you decide how to integrate suppliers are possibly number of tickets logged for the supplier, average time to log a ticket, number of updates (transactions) per ticket, maintenance cost. Irrespective of how you integrate with the suppliers, the measurement methodology will stay consistent.

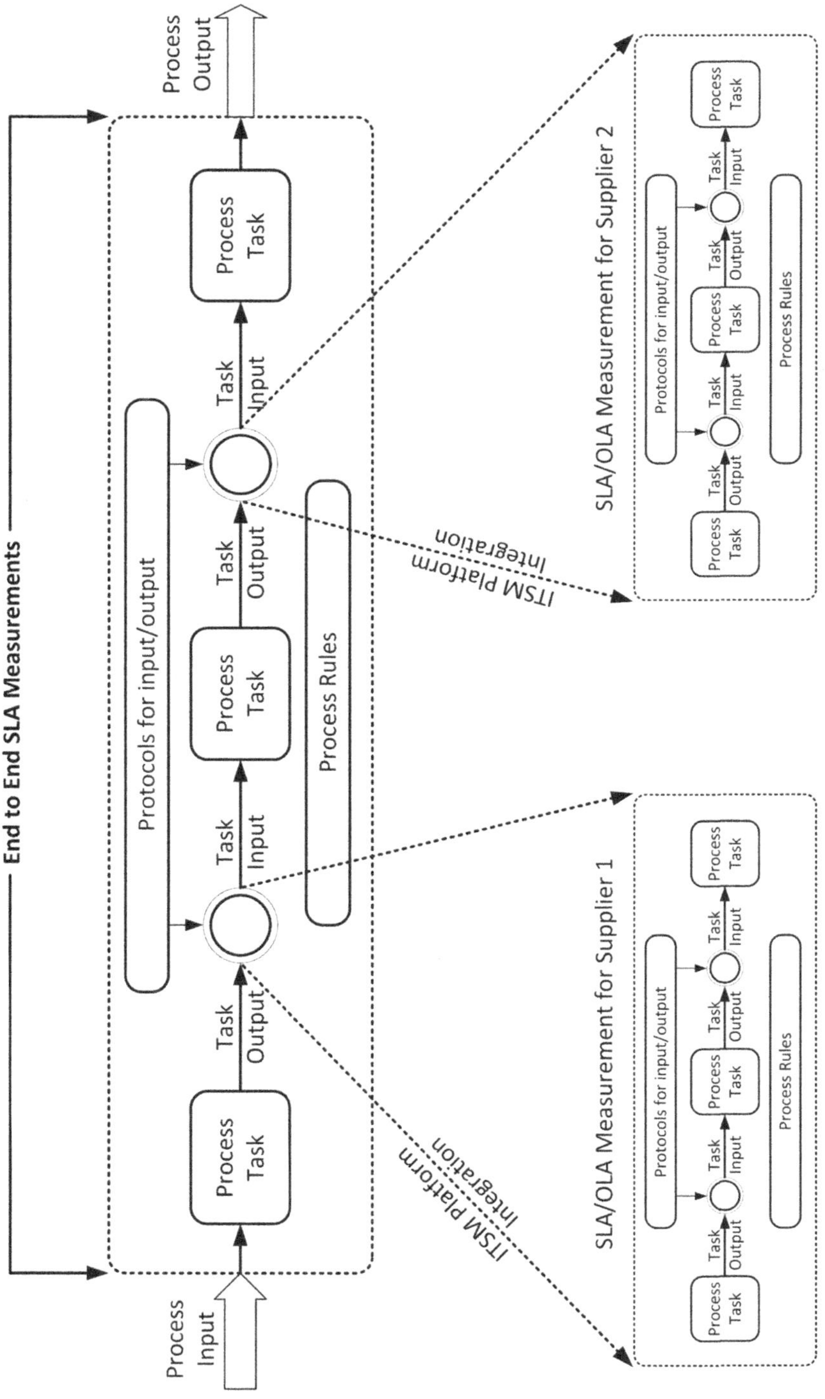

Figure 8: Process touchpoints in a multi-supplier environment

The diagram above provides a depiction of the touchpoints in a multi supplier environment and when the measurement starts and ends, both from an end to end perspective as well as the individual supplier's performance. The start and end of the process will provide the end to end SLA measurement, this is usually what the IT organization agrees with the business. So, for example, resolution of a priority 1 incident could be 2 hours, priority 2 could be 4 hours and so on. This may or may not align back to an exact SLA with the backend suppliers.

The measurement of the supplier's performance will commence from the point of assigning the ticket to them and will pause when the ticket is returned back by the supplier. This may be an update or even a resolution in many cases.

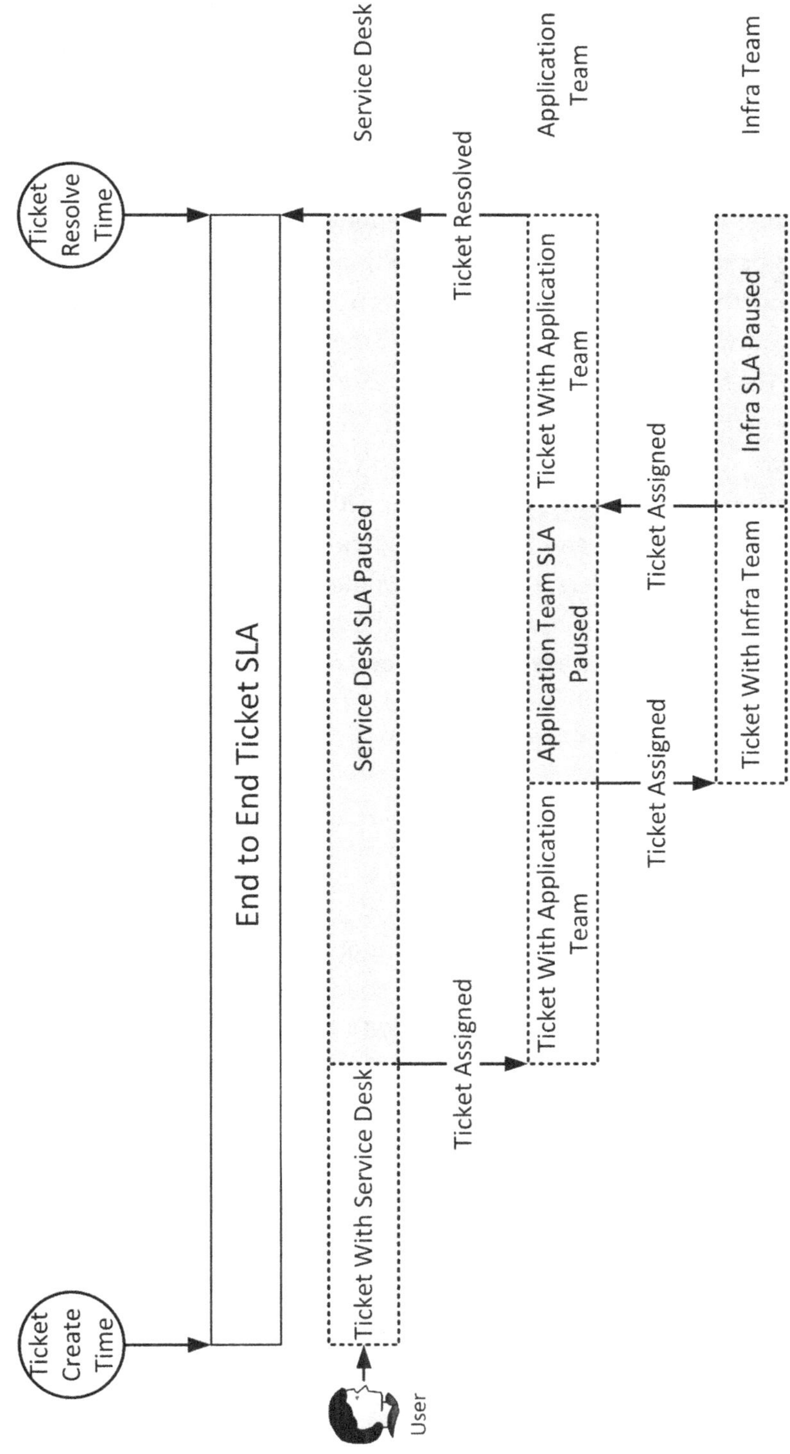

Figure 9: Measurement methodology in a multi supplier environment

Figure 9: Measurement methodology in a multi supplier environment below looks at a specific example of an incident ticket. The time that the ticket is created and resolved, will provide the end to end SLA measurement. However, each individual supplier's performance is calculated based on when they are involved. When the ticket moves out of a queue, that team's SLA is paused (note that it isn't stopped) and if the ticket were to come back into their queue, the clock continues from where it previously left off. Each individual supplier or team's performance (in our example below, that is the service desk, the application team and the infrastructure team) will be measured as a combination of the time that the ticket was assigned to them. Although we are referring to them as an SLA, assuming that these are external suppliers and are governed by a formal SLA, in the ITIL terminology, only the end to end measurement would be considered an SLA, while the suppliers agreements would be underpinning contracts and the internal teams' targets would be operational level agreements (OLA) or in some cases even a service level objective (SLO).

2.2.2 SLAs for Cloud

Immaterialism of SLAs for Cloud

Service Level Agreements (SLAs) have been in existence since IT organizations (MIS in old days) started adopting a more professional and formal approach towards IT and it soon became a core theme in traditional IT service management (ITSM). It received an extremely high level of prominence with the proliferation of ITIL and then even became an obsessive theme in outsourcing contracts.

While I am of the firm belief that most of the SLAs in traditional ITSM are meaningless, in this section, I just want to dwell on a specific point – the traditional SLA concept for cloud services are dead. So if you are thinking of defining and managing the SLA while buying cloud services, then you are wasting your time as well as the providers time.

The reason is very simple. A cloud service provider is not designing the service specifically for you, it is a standardized service. They have already built the desired level of availability and performance to compete in the marketplace and satisfy the requirements of most. It would be futile for you to seek higher availability or performance in the contractual SLA. If you are negotiating the SLA with a provider who is a "Leader" in the industry, you will not succeed and if you are negotiating with a provider who is a "Contender", they will likely sign anything to win the business; and we all know how unrealistic SLAs are written and delivered. It is an attempt to solve technology problems with legal tools. This has already been happening in managed services. Providers agree to anything, then when it moves to operations, that's when the penny drops that the service cannot meet the expectations. A legal solution cannot give you more availability when using the same technology solution. Therefore, seeking a "flexible" provider does not really make sense other than the self-satisfaction of achieving an immaterial win. If you seek the opinion of legal and financial people on the topic of negotiating SLAs, they will all provide an opinion and emphasize the importance, because this is what they have to offer as their value addition, regardless of whether it really makes a sense or not. Another misleading concept is of bringing in penalties to make SLAs better. Penalty is not a technology solution either and therefore cannot improve the SLA. In many cases, penalties are also associated with outages and unavailability of services, which translates into a loss of billing for the provider and therefore, the provider has a strong drive to restore the service as quickly as possible anyway. If you think that your penalties are making the provider work harder, that is just an illusion and by the way, the potential penalty is already buffered in the price.

So, if a focus on SLA negations is a waste of time, then what is the right approach? The right approach is to focus on the right architecture of the cloud service for your purpose. You should use the available options from the provider and configure them correctly for your need. This includes building redundancy and elasticity in your architecture to ensure the availability and performance specifically for you, while the underlying services and SLA of the provider remain a standard offering of the provider. After this, the negotiations will be just confined to the pricing and discount and that is a much simpler job for both the parties.

Service Level Management for Cloud

As we have already seen, the SLA and the process for service level management are different. Based on the discussions above, the service level management process for the cloud provider will include the following:

1. Define the market and customer
2. Understand customer and market need
3. Understand opportunities
4. Develop offering and SLA
5. Establish measurement system
6. Measure and report service level achievement
7. Fix the deficiency in delivery thru SIP (Service Improvement Plan)

When the cloud service provider's business is being set up, they are actually setting things up without any business requests. The standard offerings and associated SLAs are defined, built and published as consumable service in a catalog that can then be exposed to customers.

2.2.3 SLA in XaaS Model

"As a service" has become a fashionable term, but this has a specific connotation, which most sourcing and IT manager do not appreciate. The desire is to buy 'as a service', which basically implies the ability to scale up or down and pay based on the usage, but the requirements for a customized service still remain. This is fundamentally wrong. We have already looked at SLAs for cloud services; and that is a typical "as a service" offering. Exactly the same logic applies when you procure anything else as a service. So, what really happens in the XaaS model?

Every person in an organization or even a supplier for that matter, has to be very clear on the service that they are producing and who the customer is. If you are not able to define this, then you do not know what you are doing. In the old world, a person could have been a server administrator, in the new world, the service this same person would provide would be compute services and the customer would be the application or development teams. This would be published in a catalogue and the compute service would be available and visible only to the development teams based on the profiles. It would be a standardized service, with a predefined SLA offered by the supplier and that is all the supplier would be responsible for. This is a very common scenario with IaaS or infrastructure as a service. In the service supply chain, every actor has a defined role. We will look at the roles in the next section. In every enterprise, if you are doing something, then you are producing something, which may be a discrete service or a component within a larger service.

The IT departments in every industry, quickly jump onto the latest bandwagon and adopt buzzwords, without really understanding what they mean or how it would benefit them or even how they need to change. Lately, there has been a steep surge of discussions on the topic of 21st Century Enterprise in global forums. But what does that mean?

- Bring technology into the core of the business,
- Design cloud native service and offer everything as a service (XaaS),
- Offer service to consumers in catalog and empower them with self-service, and
- Focus on managing the outcome with the role of business orchestrator between multiple service creator and service consumers.

What does it all lead to? I see three types of emerging technology roles in the business-IT domain as enterprise move towards the XaaS era—service consumers, service creators and a service orchestrator. The enterprise would play the role of an orchestrator, and orchestrate the services from largely external service providers. This goes beyond the traditional multi supplier or SIAM function we have talked of above, because in the XaaS model, people become the last resort and most activities are automated. This will bring in the challenges in each of the following four areas:

- ***Challenge 1: Service creation challenges***
  Enterprises need to adopt radical changes during service design while taking the XaaS approach. Designing does not mean development. By design, a service must have a precisely defined 'consumption method and consumption components'. Also, the design should be self-serviceable; even break-fix ought to be self-serviceable. Besides, self-healing would also be an inherent feature of every service.
  Moreover, another design and development criterion is that every service must be ubiquitously consumable. In other words, it should be cloud-based, BYOD enabled and personalize-able for the consumers.
  New technologies are emerging and quickly gaining maturity to design and develop new services. For example, containers are their finding place in data centers, pushing down virtual machines to a layer below, in the same manner as virtual machines have pushed the application host to a layer below.

- ***Challenge 2: Service consumption challenges***
  Predominantly, what defines the service consumption is 'self-service'. 'Customers' must learn to become the new generation 'consumers' and reconcile with self-service, as assisted support becomes a thing of the past. Note that, self-support is also a part of self-service.

- ***Challenge 3: Enterprise inertia***
  The immediate challenge for the enterprises is the ability to redesign the existing service. Even though the cloud has proven its worth and is widely available, organizations are still a long way off in migrating production workloads to the cloud; some have done so, but in most large enterprises, it is typically development and test workloads.

- ***Challenge 4: Organizational change management***
  This is the most difficult part, but there is no choice. Change or be left behind.

  So, what happens to the traditional models of SLAs and OLAs? The OLA becomes irrelevant. The SLA for the service is pre-published on the catalog and standardized across customers.

2.2.3.1 Service Chain entity in XaaS model

Before we get into the XaaS model in IT, let's look at an analogy of a consumer goods delivery chain to better understand the service delivery chain entities.

Figure 10: Product delivery chain for FCMG below shows the product delivery chain entities. Each layer in the chain has a specific defined role and agreement with the previous layer in the chain. The wholesaler doesn't care about what agreement or terms the warehouse has with the factory that manufactures the product. Each entity only really cares about their relationship, terms, costs and SLAs with one level above and one level below, i.e. what do you provide and to whom, at what cost and terms at the level above and what do you receive from the level below.

Some criteria flows through the chain and may actually be provided by one of the entities only. E.g. the manufacturer's warranty. So, when the retailer sells to the consumer, should there be a defect in the product, the consumer would actually contact the creator of the product in many cases, although large scale retailers may offer for the product to be returned to them and they then send it back. But at the end of the day, the warranty on the product is provided by the manufacturer, even though someone else along the chain may provide an after-sale service. Often also referred to as flow down terms. If one entity provides an assurance, then the next entity provides the same and it flows up, as well as down the chain and eventually ends at the manufacturer.

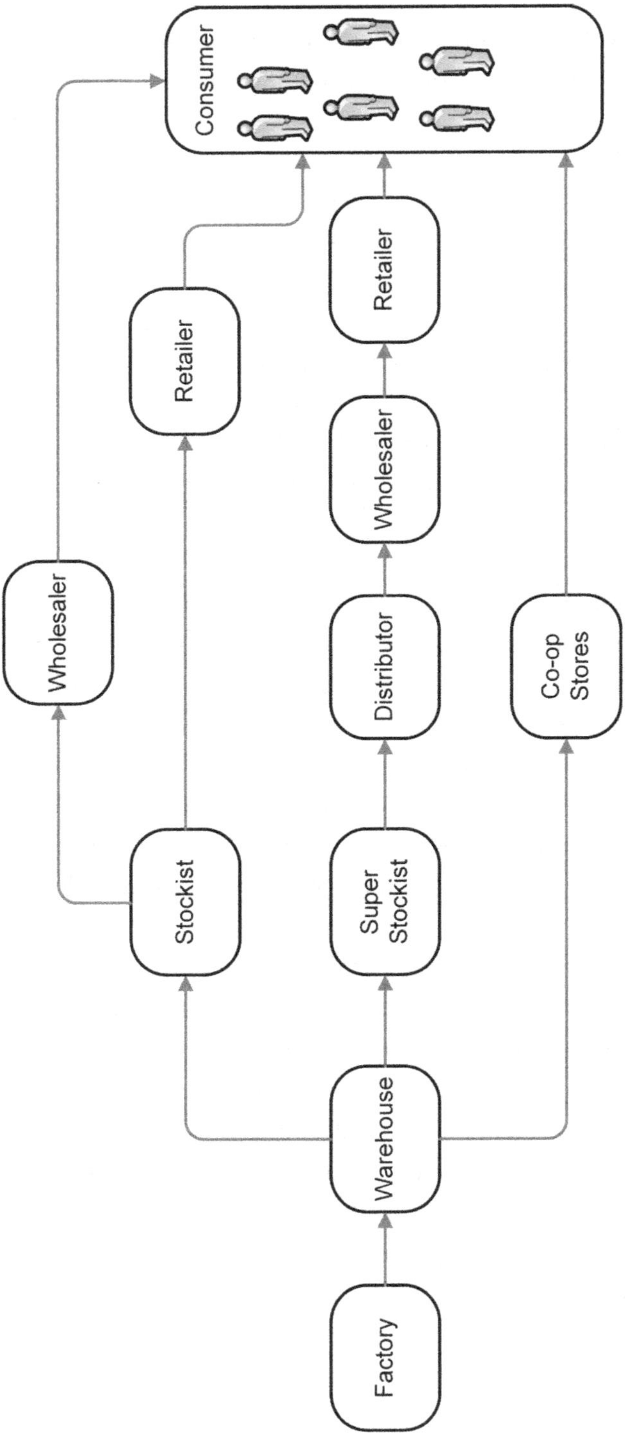

Figure 10: Product delivery chain for FCMG

Another entity may of course up the ante and guarantee the product for a longer length of time, for example extended product warranty, also called service warranty. This is in addition to the standard warranty on new items. The extended warranty may be offered by the warranty administrator, the retailer or the manufacturer. This is also sometimes done to encourage customers to buy from them as the product is also available elsewhere

How does the above example differ when you are delivering services? There is no warehouse where you can store these and sell them on at a later date! What happens if it is IT services? *Figure 11: Service delivery chain* below looks at the entities that we see today in the delivery chain of IT services:

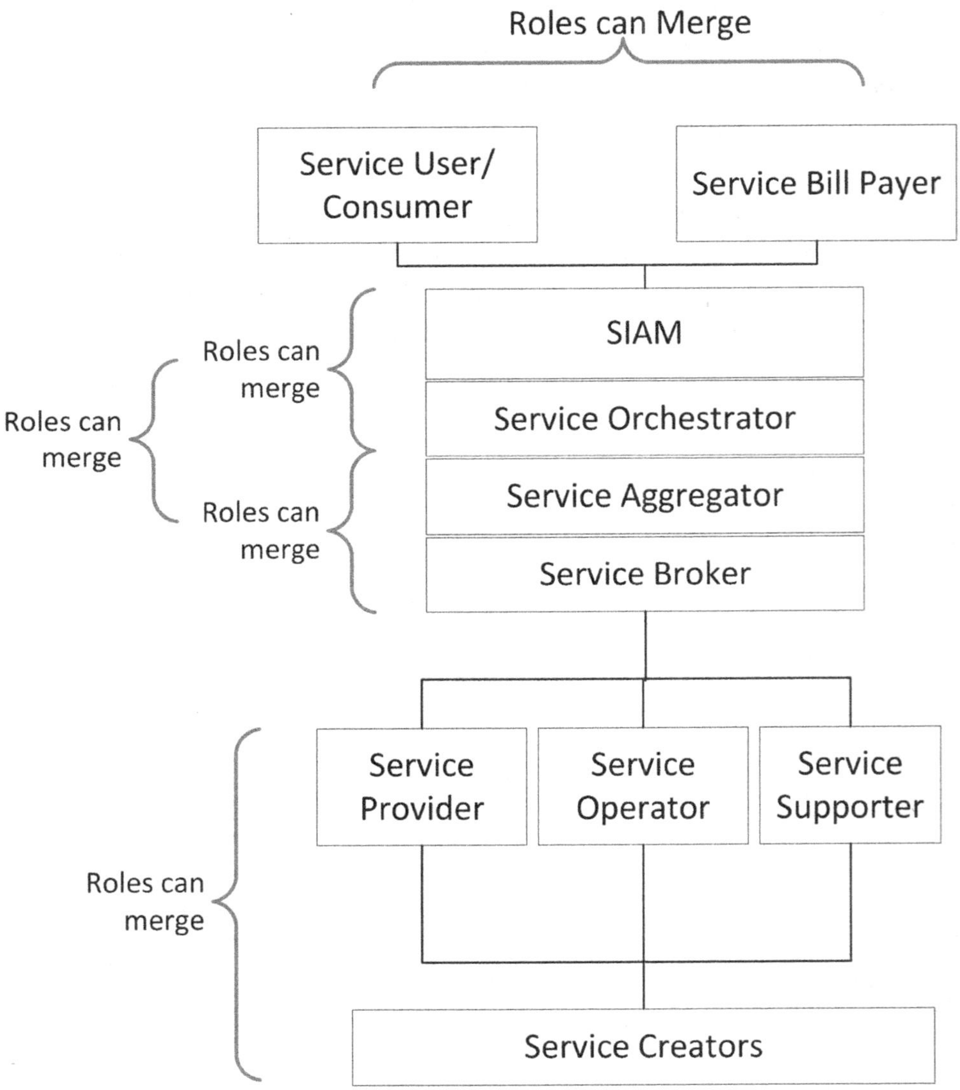

Figure 11: Service delivery chain

The first thing you will notice is that ITIL actually doesn't mention any of the above roles in its framework and process models. So let's clarify what each does:

- Service Creator is the entity that creates or produces the service.
- Service Operator is the entity that maintains or keeps the service in a usable state
- Service Provider is the entity that takes it further - either to the consumer or to the other entity in the chain
- Service Supporter is the entity that provides the break fix support for the service
- Service Broker is the commercial mediator entity for the service
- Service Aggregator is the consolidating entity without altering the individual service. It can however also be a combination of multiple discrete service, or the consumer can be using an individual service.
- Service Orchestrator is the service delivery integration entity and makes the individual service non-visible to the consumer
- Service Integrator is the service delivery as well as service support integration entity that is the final interface to the consumer and payer

It is important to note that multiple roles can be merged – for example the broker and aggregator role can be played by the same entity, or one single entity could play the roles of broker, aggregator, orchestrator and integrator. Similarly, the creator could also be the provider, operator and supporter.

Another important point to note is that every service does not need to pass through every role in the service delivery chain. Many services can directly be consumed without any layers like the aggregator or orchestrator.

The criteria to measure performance and the SLAs are dependent on the type of service that is being delivered. Some services will be measured by their usability *(think of "DropBox" as a storage service, or a corporate communications solution like Skype there is no physical product and the measure of performance will be how usable it is).* Each roles customer is different and the SLAs along the chain will also vary.

To summarize the different models and how SLAs, OLA's and UC's would be applicable, refer to the table below:

	Legacy ITIL	Multi Supplier	XaaS
Roles	• Service Provider • Internal Groups • External Supplier	• Managed Service Providers • Internal Group • External Supplier (Products) • Sub-Contractors	• Service Supply Chain (Creator, Operator, Provider, Supporter, Broker, Integrator, Orchestrator)
	• SLA	• EU-SLA • SLA(n1-nx)	• SLA
	• OLA	• Internal OLA • External OLA • Implied OLA	• N/A
	• UC	• UC • Delegated UC	• N/A

Table 3: Delivery Models - applicability of SLAs, OLAs & UCs

2.2.4 SLA for Security

When does security becomes a nuisance?

Security is meant to provide a blissful and secure feeling. In the enterprise, in my opinion, it is getting to a stage where it has a nuisance value. I do not disagree that it is required, but how much security is good enough? There is nothing like absolute or guaranteed security. Security is always in the context of a risk appetite. Security departments and suppliers have a vested interest in minimizing the risk appetite in order to inflate their artificial value and importance in the organization. Security becomes a nuisance when the risk management approach is pushed in the background and the control agenda comes to the forefront. The right approach is to consult the business for the risk appetite and design the security policies accordingly, however, in most cases security policies are built and enforced unilaterally. The reality however is that a business cannot progress if they do not take a certain amount of risk. Security can in many cases be pulling in the opposite direction. Security is a sacred cow. It doesn't matter what you really think, you just cannot be the one who can argue or go against security recommendations or take a call to overrule them.

In my professional career, as an end user, I have had to deal with a fair share of organizational security policies. Some of these have been related to email, especially on my mobile device or with storage on the cloud, as this supposedly introduces a high security risk. The same policies however do not apply when the information or email is accessed from a laptop. I understand and already know that a mobile is a small device and can be lost a lot easier as compared to a laptop, but not allowing me to copy text from my email into another app just doesn't make sense to me. If someone has found my phone, been able to get past my fingerprint or password login and then managed to access my email, what will you achieve by preventing them from copying text into another application on the device? This does nothing to increase security. My only interpretation of this security policy is that the organization doesn't trust their employees and thinks that a corporate email is going to be copied and sent via a chat application! Did they forget that I could actually forward the email itself to someone else! Beggars belief! All it does is reduce my productivity and level of annoyance!

Confidentiality, integrity and availability, also known as the CIA triad, is a model designed to guide policies for information security within an organization. Confidentiality is a set of rules that limits access to information to people that are authorized, integrity is the assurance that the information is trustworthy and accurate, and availability is a guarantee of reliable access to the information by authorized people. In my little rant above of copying data from my email application on my phone, the security department actually restricts my access to the information, so aren't they actually going against the whole security principle and compromising availability? Their desire to control data (for no logical outcome) also negatively impacts the accessibility and is actually countering the intent of any SLA. Confidentiality doesn't mean anti-availability, I have checked the dictionary. Oh, I wasn't aware security had their own!

Security is not able to sign an SLA for outcome, i.e. guaranteed security. All of the activities and control (i.e. the output) cannot guarantee an outcome, then what is the point of the output in the first place? The sole outcome is to lull the organization into a false sense of security!

We are also drowning in the name of security best practice. Yes, when you move to the cloud, you are trusting a 3rd party with your information and would need to have some assurance that controls are in place to protect the data. But, for a recent engagement, a client provided me with an excel spreadsheet that had 133 controls and security requirements, which they had downloaded from a security alliance site. It didn't matter if any of them were really a requirement or provided any real security or even any consideration on what role the client also had to play in securing their information, it was left solely on the supplier to "comply" or be "penalized". We have stopped talking like grown-ups and it is all about covering our backs. Doing the right things as opposed to doing things right.

It is not just internal security departments, many organizations are also subject to regulatory compliance in business sectors, but applying such data protection legislation can become a nightmare. Sarbanes-Oxley in the United States and the General Data Protection Regulations (GDPR) in the European Union.

It is important that the decision makers are properly informed of the aspects, pitfalls and benefits of each approach before signing a contract. When outsourcing, a service level agreement (SLA) helps to spell out those details.

A security service provider's capability usually include monitoring firewalls, intrusion-detection systems, analyzing the outputs of logs and carrying out configuration management for devices and software that they are responsible for. They are responsible to ultimately prevent, remediate and recover from security incidents. So rather than dictating what tools, IDS or procedures are deployed, wouldn't it make more sense to just agree how quickly they will respond when things go pear shaped? After all we have hopefully already agreed that there is no such thing as guaranteed security, so things will go wrong.

2.3 Types of Services and SLAs

Service delivery SLAs and service support SLAs

IT service delivery refers to the kind of service where there is no direct interaction between the service producer and service receiver. Services are produced by machines and delivered to receivers via network channels on the receivers' devices. Of course, there are people at both ends. At the service-production end, people operate the machines that produce the service. At the receiver end, a person interacts with his or her device to use the service. Thus, IT service delivery is machine-to-machine interaction, with a person behind the machine at each end.

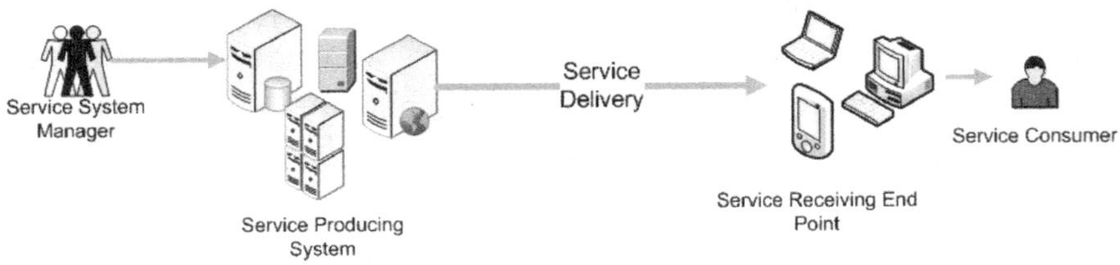

Figure 12: Service Delivery

In ITIL, availability management, capacity management, and service-level management processes are key service delivery processes.

As we can see illustrated Figure 12: Service Delivery , machines perform the prime activity of service delivery, and people (service providers) manage those machines. Machines interface with the customer, with people in this background.

This situation gives relatively clear definitions of standards and targets. Processes of production can be effective and leave little scope of deviation from written specifications. The quality is relatively easy to define and achieve. The quality aspect of the service is the **technical quality:** measuring *what* the customer was left with when the service was delivered. A major proportion of designing SLAs for this is devoted to define these aspects of services, because it is easy to articulate this. Also, much of the service-level management activities are focused on this aspect because they are do-able. The complexity is related to the technology and hard skills that are required for quality delivery. The quality dimensions are reliability, efficiency, performance, completeness, integrity, fault tolerance, and tangibility.

Service support refers to the kind of service where there is a direct interaction between the service provider and service receiver. This need usually arises when the service receiver is not able to use the service (i.e. when there is an incident). Inability to use does not necessarily mean the service is not delivered. It is just that support is required. If the delivery of service is interrupted, service support will be a catalyst to restore the service delivery.

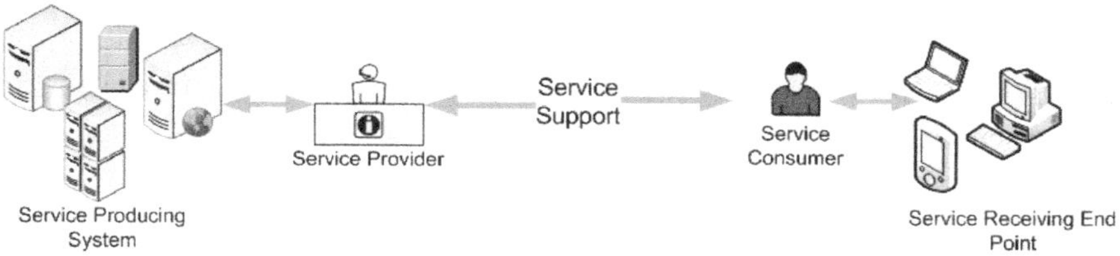

Figure 13: Service Support

In ITIL, incident management, problem management, and change management are key service-support processes. People perform the prime activity of service support, and the customer directly receives the benefit. Here people are dealing with people, and machines are in the background. This is a slightly more complex situation from a standards and definition point of view. Consistency is extremely difficult due to several uncontrollable factors. The quality of service is determined by human factors. Since the human factors exist on both sides (service provider and receiver), the dependency on the human factor is extremely high. Standardization is much harder to achieve. In other words, there is a significant scope of deviation from subjective definitions.

The quality of such aspect of service is the **functional quality**—measuring how the customer received the service. The complexity is all about human behaviors, and soft skills are extremely important to accomplish quality service. The quality dimensions governing this aspect of service are responsiveness, courtesy, communication, understanding customers, confidentiality, and emotional resonance.

Transaction-Based Service (Ticket based SLAs)

There are several SLAs that are based on transaction-based services. Examples are Incident Resolution and Request Fulfilment. A transaction ticket is created to manage the service delivery lifecycle. When the service delivery chain has multiple groups, the ticket tracking system can track and measure the performance of each participant in the chain. SLAs/OLAs for such situation are easy to define and implement.

All the services that can be identified, isolated, and contained in a specific instance are referred as transaction-based services. Characteristics of transaction-based services are listed below:

1. Ticket-based
2. Finite life cycle
3. Repetitive instances of same process via different transactions
4. Integral status tracking and easy measurements
5. High visibility

Services delivered as "support" services are usually transaction-based. That means each "piece" of service is measured by a transaction. The most prominent examples of this are IMAC (install, move, add, change) requests (service requests) and incident-resolution services. Other prominent processes to manage this kind of service are event management, change management, and problem management. A customer requests a particular service item. The service providers deliver that particular service item, and the transaction closes.

Perpetual services

Perpetual services are, on the other hand, continuously running streams of services, and you tap them when you need them. Examples of this service are web services and e-mail services. The major difference between these two is the service-management process and corresponding measurements. Transaction-based services are normally measured from an elapsed time or duration perspective, while perpetual services are measured from availability and throughput criteria. Service delivery processes, such as availability-management processes and capacity-management processes, are meant for perpetual services.

Non-Ticketed SLAs

There are several collaborative situations to enable delivery of services, which are not measured by transactions. Examples of such situations are providing some information, or some data or some report from one group to another to enable the service delivery from another group. These kinds of SLA/OLA are difficult to define and even more difficult to measure. "*The manner in which a group will interact and collaborate*" section of the OLA attempts to define this. Regular meetings between the groups and minutes of the meeting that form part of the governance could be the criteria used to measure performance and compliance of the agreed OLA.

2.3.1 SLA and RACI

Services are delivered by execution of activities, which can be executed by machines or people. Each of these activities has to be defined and decided by someone, irrespective if it is finally executed by a machine or human. Each activity will have a "what" and "who". These are very critical. The "what is to be delivered" relates to the "accountability", while the "who" relates to the responsibility. No service can be produced if the "R" and "A" role are not defined. There are other people or systems that may be informed or consulted along the way, but these are optional and may or may not exist for every service.

If you can't measure, then you can't manage it. Every service, will have to be managed, and therefore measured. Every service will have an SLA or an SLO. A target must exist. But as we have seen, each service has someone who is accountable and someone or something which is responsible for the execution and delivery of the activities or the tasks. In conclusion, every SLA will have someone who is accountable and responsible. Therefore "R" and "A" are the mandatory parts of every SLA, while "C" and "I" can be optional or a nice to have.

I have come across many competitive bids, where the advisor to the client provide an Request for Proposal (RFP) document that already lists out what the supplier is to provide and the response from the supplier is only a "yes or no" against each task to confirm if they are compliant or not. Unfortunately, every task is basically pointing towards outsourcing of the responsibility of delivery, but when you look at the SLA sheet, it indicates they are asking for SLA for accountability.

Could there also be an SLA when you are consulted or informed? It could be that you are not responsible or accountable for any of the delivery or support activities, but could there be situations where information is required (consulted) for the actual outcome? For example, when the business provides a forecast and the client is required to help translate that into IT capacity requirements? I haven't seen a lot of these in my interactions with clients.

2.3.2 SLA for task vs SLA for results

Output vs Outcome

Output relates to the deliverables produced by tasks or activities, while the outcome relates to the benefits or the results of producing the output – or the consequence of the output. The outcome is at a higher level and may require output from not just one but multiple activities and tasks. Outputs, such as revenue and profit, enable us to fund outcomes; but without outcomes, there is no need for outputs.

SLAs are often set for the task and thus for the output rather than for the result or outcome because it is easy to do so. Let us look at some examples below:

- Incident management SLA will contain break-fix or resolution as the output but improvement in the productivity of a user is the actual outcome.
- Request fulfillment for delivery of a server within a predefined time, is the output of a task, but the usability of the server for a development team will require additional activities of storage allocation, installation of a development environment, network connectivity, etc.; i.e. an "environment"; so the outcome may require multiple outputs to actually deliver an outcome

  Security is another interesting domain. Most organizations will typically negotiate an SLA for installation of security patches within x number of days of their release, or how quickly a security incident is responded to or an SLA for distribution of virus definitions, installation, etc. Where is the SLA for security achieved and how will it be measured?

One output can result into one or more outcome; conversely multiple outputs may be required to create an outcome. Historically, most enterprise IT outsourcing contracts have focused on SLAs for the output of activities (resolution of incidents, fulfilment of requests, etc.). The trend off late has been for enterprise IT to ask for *"business outcomes"* rather than output driven SLAs. The approach has mostly been to address tactical tasks and therefore tactical SLAs, rather than strategic SLAs or outcomes. With the phenomenal leaps in technology and the way enterprise IT applications are now developed (micro services, built on a platform, delivered over the cloud, as a service, etc.), it is now a lot easier to define and agree SLAs that are outcome based.

2.3.3 Operational SLA vs strategic SLA

Everyone talks about strategy. It is a highly misused and abused term. The original context of the term was the planning and directing overall military operations and movements in a war or battle. Sometimes, you had to lose the battle to win the war. In chess, pawns are sacrificed to get into a better position to attack the king. Strategy in enterprise and business terms is defined as a plan of action designed to achieving a long-term or overall aim. It will exist in the background and all the activities and tasks (output) and their resultant outcomes are all meant to serve the long-term goal and aim.

Operational SLAs are tied to the output of activities or tasks. They may of course be related to a strategic objective or service. While strategic SLAs are tied to the outcomes of a strategic service. When a strategic SLA is designed, it is done with an outcome in mind, not the method of delivery.

It is also quite possible that there could be a conflict at times between the operational and strategic SLAs. For example, if an organizations strategy is drive more self-service, this may have an SLA for the percentage of users that are actively raising incidents or consuming services via the self-service portal. In parallel, the operational SLA for answering the phone at the service desk will be longer or less aggressive, it could also have no agreed target for the average call handling time with an aggressive first contact resolution. What this will do is cause the service desk to take a long time to answer, keep the user on the phone longer to achieve the FCR. It may lead to a bad user experience when calling the service desk, but in reality, what this is doing is encouraging users to instead access the self-service portal. This will support the achievement of the strategic SLA as well as the organizational strategy. You must sometimes lose the battle to win the war.

2.3.4 SLA for proactive Services

Another abused term is "proactive". How do you define "pro-activeness"? It is basically addressing something before it happens. So how do you anticipate issues? There are several ways it could be done:

• Sensory System: People also call it a gut feeling. We receive a sensory warning from colleagues, customers and from within ourselves. We sense the symptoms around us like the changing attitude of customers, increased stress level, declining morale etc.

- Statistical data: If we analyze call data, problem records and various statistical reports we will likely be able to identify trends and possible issues ahead of time.
- Internal Factors: If we are aware of the company's IT strategy and IT plans, we can predict the service needs ahead of time.
- External factors: Industry trends, technology trends and vendor reports will assist in making intelligent predictions.

Although we may anticipate that something may go wrong, the characteristics of proactive support can be defined as:

- Taking an initiative
- Fixing things before they break
- Maintaining an improvement cycle or continuous service improvement

If you cannot pre-define what "taking an initiative" is, how would you measure it? It may be possible to measure and identify something it breaks using analytics and events, but other criteria like taking an initiative or the extent of initiate isn't possible.

Defining the characteristics is easier than negotiating an SLA or creating a methodology to measure it. Just because it is fashionable to talk about being proactive, doesn't mean it automatically equates to it being part of a service or with an associated SLA. The SLA agreed by the service provider is to deliver the service and as long as it meets the agreed targets, there is no obligation to improve it any further. Customers tend to ask for an SLA for proactiveness, it should be at the discretion of the service provider. Customer's think that proactive support usually benefits the service provider as it may reduce their risk of breaching SLAs or the amount of effort required to support or deliver the service. But, being proactive comes at a cost. An airline may decide to upgrade you to a higher class of travel. They typically use a combination of the fare class and your loyalty status to decide who gets bumped up to the next class. It is however at the discretion of the airline and depends entirely on their circumstances. You cannot pay for an economy class seat and demand to get the leg room or meal from business class. Similarly, proactive support is a privilege of the service consumer, not a right. It is entirely at the discretion of the provider if he is proactive or not. You could of course pay and then demand for proactivity! The human tendency however is to always demand for more, even when you are not entitled to it. On a lighter note, let me tell you a joke. There was a street market, but it was well known that to get the best prices you had to bargain. A local resident who was well versed with the ways of the sellers and the haggling, said to his friend who was visiting, "the guiding principle is, whatever the seller quotes, you should ask for the product at half the price". With this important lesson learnt, the friend proceeded to get himself some good deals. At the market, he enquired about the cost of an umbrella. On being told, it was priced at $16, he said, I will give you $8. The seller reluctantly agreed. The man then asked for it for $4, after much haggling, the seller again agreed. The man then again said no, "I will only pay $2". This went on until he was offered the umbrella for free, the man refused, and said I want 2 for free! Asking for proactive SLAs is like asking for another one for free!

2.4 SLA Management vs Service Level Management

Both, the process of service level management and management of SLAs are considerably underestimated in most of the IT organizations. Most tools have the capability to monitor the SLA in operations and send notifications. This is usually named as the SLM module in the tool and has conditioned the mind of IT professionals to think that service level management is tracking the SLA in operations.

Service level management is an exhaustive process that starts with understanding the service level requirements in the beginning of the service design phase itself. The key SLM activities include:

1. Define service level requirements (SLR)
2. Evaluate SLR and benchmark against the delivery capabilities

3. Build the capabilities or recalibrate the requirements
4. Negotiate SLA
5. Negotiate OLA and UC
6. Establish measurement system
7. Measure and report service level achievement
8. Fix the deficiency in delivery through SIP (Service Improvement Plan)

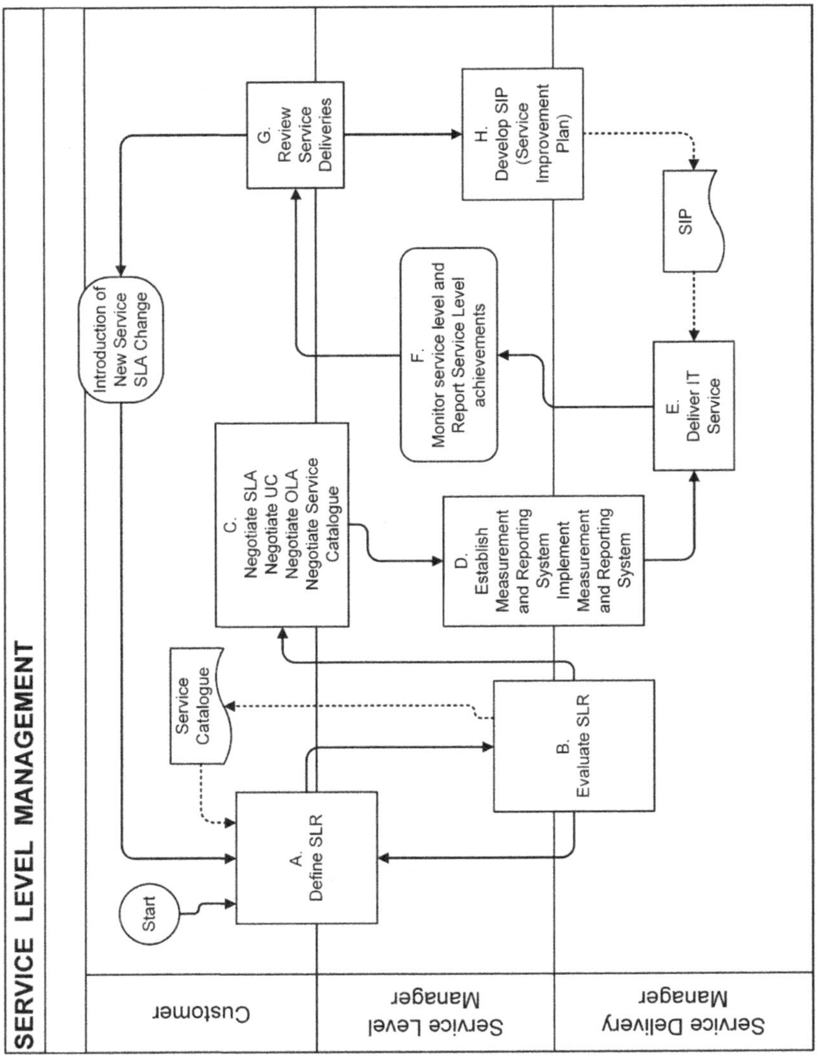

Figure 14: Service Level Management

The operational activities surrounding the measurement and tracking of SLA in operation and triggering the corrective actions (tracking the incident resolution time in the incident management lifecycle) is deemed as service level management, although it is a small part of the much larger SLA management process.

SLA management focuses on the SLA maintenance which means the assurance that SLA is meaningful, business aligned, complete and can indeed serve as the reference document surrounding the service delivery activities. SLA management is also responsible to maintain the integrity of SLAs and the interpretation of SLAs are not distorted. In summary, it is the measuring, tracking, tweaking and reporting of SLAs. It is a subset of the overall service level management process, which covers the definition and negotiating of SLAs.

Institutionalization of SLAs

An organization I once consulted, had outsourced infrastructure to a well-known IT supplier. There were approximately 30 SLA which attracted penalties if breached and 127 KPI's that didn't. In total, 157 targets that had to be measured, met, analyzed, improved and governed by the client too. Several of them were sensible and related to availability of services, fair enough. Some were SLAs for SLAs, e.g.: "SLA reports delivered on time". Another was "Number of defined SLAs breached" which strangely did attract a penalty if breached! So you got penalized for breaching SLAs and then got penalized again for breaching them! There were others like "% of change performed during working and non-working hours", when it was the client who was approving the changes! Many couldn't be understood by most, measured or even challenged, for example 'for all severity "X" non-cyclic job failures, the monitoring team should follow up with the resolver AFTER receiving acknowledgment they are addressing the failure'. I had to read this a few times to understand what it was meant to do, but couldn't work out the objective of it. So you follow up with the resolver after they have acknowledged receiving the ticket? A bit like sending an email, receiving a reply that they have received and are addressing it and then calling up and asking if they are working on it. What a waste of time, effort and money. The supplier would meet the SLA, as he just had to throw bodies at the requirement which the client ultimately paid for! Another strange one was "Number of agreed reports rejected due to inaccurate data". The client didn't have any alternate source of data anyway, so had to rely on the information generated by the supplier, basically the same one that the reports were generated from. Effectively, this SLA couldn't be accurately executed anyway. I wonder who defines these SLAs, is it the advisor, is it the IT or service managers or all of them. Eventually, after several sensible meetings, the 157 were reduced to 30 that actually mattered.

Listed below are some other common hurdles with SLAs in most organizations:

- SLAs not properly communicated: if the SLAs are not communicated correctly, users will create their own set of expectations; eventually, it doesn't matter if the supplier does meet their SLA, it will likely not meet what the users think they were supposed to receive.
- SLA IT based instead of business aligned: We have already seen some weird and wonderful SLAs being defined in the paragraph above. Setting very IT focused SLAs instead of what the business wants or even needs. One example I came across was "% of the number of agreed recommendations made by Capacity Management are acted upon". Shouldn't this actually be related to business demand?
- SLAs too lengthy: Here is an example – "For all Supplier controlled equipment, the Supplier will be responsible for ensuring that the latest Anti-Virus signatures are deployed on at least 95% of devices within 24 hours and 100% within 5 working days. Security Patches shall be deployed on at least 95% of devices within the timescales agreed at the Threats and Vulnerabilities Forum and 100% within 90 days, unless the device is classified as a part of the PCI DSS scope in which case the patches must be applied within the Threats and Vulnerability Forum

timescales. In order for equipment to be temporary excluded from measurement then documented and tolerated risks (tolerated by client) must be in place." Be honest, how many time did you have to read this SLA to understand what was meant to be done and how would you propose this is measured using system defined timestamps?

- SLM seen as overhead rather than as impacting service: the service level management can be easily perceived as an unnecessary overhead, if the SLAs do not actually provide any tangible information to measure the service being provided or allowing any informed decision making.
- SLM used for contract arbitration rather than for relationship building: This is probably one of the most common issues in most organizations. The SLM process used to arbitrate contracts; it doesn't matter if the supplier meets the SLA or not. If they don't, then the client has the leverage and if they do meet the SLA, then it is deemed that the SLA was too lenient and stretched targets need to be set to really show an improvement in the service.
- Dealing with legacy contracts: technology evolves, business needs and requirements change, but long-term contracts may be difficult to amend. Additionally, bringing in new suppliers may introduce new SLAs, but how they align to existing suppliers' contracts could also pose a challenge.
- Verbal agreements/expectations: not everything can be captured in a contract. Requirements, decisions, agreements, implied and assumed conclusions are all part of a normal business relationship. But delivering on them could be a different matter entirely
- Unrealistic targets: I won't say anything more on this!
- SLA based on desire rather than achievable targets: My mess for less is common. The impractical expectation of achieving SLAs that have never been done before but using the same existing architecture and technology solutions are even more common.
- Inadequate focus, resources and time: just defining an SLA isn't enough; the supplier may produce all the metrics but managing that output and making decisions based on that requires resources and time. In many organizations, this is done on a best effort basis as other things priority.

- Not enough seniority for SLM: negotiating SLAs, questioning requirements and demands requires seniority.
- Responsibilities not clearly defined: achieving SLAs requires all parties to play their part. It is not just down to the supplier. If the responsibilities and dependencies are not clearly defined, there is little chance of success.

2.4.1 Managing SLA vs managing vendor

A well-managed vendor relationship will always result in increased value for both parties, a higher customer satisfaction, reduced costs as you work together and a higher quality of service from the vendor. Issues with the service will When and if problems arise, rest assured that a well-managed vendor will be quick to address the situation.

The vendor management process and function enables an organization to build strong relationships with their suppliers and service providers for the benefit of both parties. The supplier also needs to make a profit. Vendor management is not about negotiating the lowest price possible or push the vendor to deliver it at a loss, but constantly working together to deliver value and support the business. There are some key aspects to good vendor management:

- Be forthcoming with relevant information: It is important to share information with your vendors. As your business changes and your priorities need to be realigned, if your service providers are better informed, it will help them give you the tools and ability to transform.
- Treat them with respect: Understand and appreciate that the supplier is a partner along your journey. They are not a lowly servant to serve at a low price.
- Listen: If a vendor supplies a key part or service to your operation, invite that vendor to strategic meetings and let them provide you with advice and assist with your strategy. Keep in mind that they are involved with lots of other clients, have far more expertise in their area than you do and are in a better position to guide you. After all, isn't that why you

selected them in the first place?

This isn't the same as monitoring, measuring and governing the SLA performance! Reviewing, amending and tweaking the SLA achievements is of course is an important activity that is carried out by the vendor management office, but it is not managing of the vendor.

How the service management office that manages delivery of services interfaces and works together with the vendor management office is depicted below:

Service Management Office	Vendor Management Office
Chair service provider review meetings	Participate in service provider review meetings
Consolidate SLA and performance reports across the service providers	Consume the SLA reports to determine service credits
Analyse and compare performance between service providers	Release payments for processed invoices
Recommend revised SLAs/KPI's and amendments to service provider contracts	Own negotiation with service provider's on areas of improvement and new performance targets

Figure 15: SMO and VMO

2.4.2 SLA maintenance

Business requirements will change over time. This will lead to the service requirements also needing alignment and amendments, impacting previously agreed targets and SLAs. There is a need to maintain and update SLAs just like you would any other component in the environment. Even if your SLA doesn't change, over a period of time, the metrics, how you measure them or represent and report them are likely to change. So even metrics need a level of maintenance. Metrics often become obsolete. As the organization achieves higher levels of process and matures, metrics usually require change to keep pace. Good metrics reflect the reality of the current process objectives. When the organization releases new services there may be a need to measure specific parameters during early life support or until you get to a period of stability. But once you have crossed that, you could retire those measurements, as they would not be needed any more.

2.5 Can SLA achievement deliver CSAT?

Achieving the SLA does not guarantee the achievement of customer satisfaction. You can deliver a much higher level of service than the SLA mandates and still get the customer dissatisfied. The opposite is also true - you can deliver substandard services and still receive a high customer satisfaction rating. Customer satisfaction is not a matter of meeting or not meeting the SLA, rather CSAT is a matter of meeting or not meeting the expectations, that has nothing to do with the SLA. Communicating the SLA does help to setting the right expectation,

But, does customer satisfaction really matter? Well, I believe that it does not, so long as you have customer loyalty. Loyalty is priceless. If you aim for customer loyalty, customer satisfaction comes along too. People often link customer satisfaction with loyalty, but it isn't correct. There are methods to keep customers loyal, even though they may be dissatisfied, and we see this used very effectively by the airline and hotel industry.

However, it is also true that a satisfied customer can be made loyal far more easily than a dissatisfied one. So we cannot completely ignore customer satisfaction.

Before you attempt to improve customer satisfaction, you must first know who the customer is and what service they expect. This is very important because you may be targeting the wrong customer or delivering the wrong service.

In the context of enterprise service management, a service provider has two classes of service consumers – users and customers. Users use the service and customers pay for the service. A customer may or may not be a user and both have different criteria for satisfaction. User satisfaction is one of the criteria of customer satisfaction. In all engagements, the service desk agents address user satisfaction while the Account Manager aims at customer satisfaction. In the subsequent discussion, we shall call them both a customer.

The Importance of Customer Expectation

An important point to note is that customer satisfaction is NOT a matter of meeting or exceeding the SLA. It is a matter of meeting or exceeding the expectation, regardless of the SLA. It is quite possible to exceed an SLA yet fail on customer satisfaction just because the customer's expectation was larger than the SLA; conversely, we could receive customer appreciation for the service that has breached the SLA just by managing the expectation appropriately.

If we do not do anything to set the expectation, then it will be set by default and that may impact customer satisfaction. That means, setting the right SLA is the first important thing to do, communicating is the second and delivering the service as per the SLA is the third!

How to set the right customer expectations

Communicate, communicate, and communicate – this is most important when setting the expectation. In the user service process, this can be automated via e-mail communications. The system can dynamically calculate the resolution time according to the SLA and proactively communicate it. In customer relationship management, the account manager has regular discussions on the continued relevance of the SLA and has the opportunity to set the right expectations.

2.5.1 Moment of truth for CSAT

The moment of truth is the point of interaction between a service provider and customer. Jan Carlzon, the President of Scandinavian Airlines, popularized this term in 1980. He successfully steered the company out from huge losses and made it profitable by consistently high customer satisfaction rating. Jan believed that each moment of truth was an opportunity to either satisfy or dissatisfy the customer. The cumulating of moments of truth constitutes service delivery as far as customers are concerned as that is all that is visible to them. Continual management of customer expectations and perceptions means that the service provider staff must exhibit the appropriate behaviors and attitudes at each moment of truth. It is these demonstrated behaviors and attitudes that underpin a service culture.

Historically the service desk has acted as the single point of contact for end users, so they have been the epicenter for the moment of truth. But slowly, with the advancement of cognitive technology, this is slowly being taken over by machines. The users experience with the software, any people involved in the chain and the overall service will together contribute to the overall customer satisfaction. In an end to end service, there are multiple and continual moments of truth for customer experience and therefore satisfaction. Let's look at an example outside of IT to understand this better. It is not just the initial contact, but every time there is interaction with the customer. When you travel from one country to another by with an airline, you will have used multiple individual services, which could each provide a different level of satisfaction and experience. There is a moment of truth when buying the ticket, checking in at the airport, boarding the flight, did you find space above your seat to put your luggage in the overhead compartment, the ambience and temperature on the flight, the service on the flight by the cabin crew, did the flight depart on time, did your bags arrive? What if they were lost, but the airline was sympathetic and managed to locate it, you may still have a good overall experience and satisfaction. Or they weren't too compassionate and in spite of everything going well until that moment at the baggage carousel, your satisfaction would be very low!

2.6 KPI and SLA

A Key Performance Indicator (KPI) is a measurable unit to gauge how effectively a process, function or service is achieving its intended objectives. A KPI doesn't attract penalties if breached, those are typically associated with SLAs. It is quite common to find SLAs backed up by a string of KPI's. This allows you to break it down into parts and measure each individual part. It helps in identifying what part needs to be tweaked to achieve or improve performance with an SLA.

Just like an SLA, for a KPI to be effective, it must be clearly defined and quantifiable, with an agreed measurement methodology, source of data for measurement, be communicated and also align to achieving a goal. You will notice, a lot of the activities you would expect when designing SLAs also apply to KPIs.

To look at an example, it is common in IT to measure the hop count of incidents. This is done to get an early warning sign if no support group is taking responsibility for an issue. It however doesn't have any direct relation to the SLA of incident resolution. But it aligns the process and enables you to identify early on if there is an issue. There may be a valid reason for the ticket passing too. Similarly, CPU or memory utilization do not constitute unavailability when looking at performance SLAs but could provide an early warning sign of an issue to come.

KPIs should be defined for both internal and external teams. External KPIs relate to and support external SLAs, while the internal KPIs are an indicator of performance, but do not translate to SLAs.

2.6.1 If there is KPI, there ought to be CSF as well

To achieve any KPI or even SLA for that matter, there are certain critical success factors (CSF), or things that must be in place for there to be a chance of success. It is important to understand what these are, because without it, we are setting the delivery teams up for failure.

Let's look at Incident Management, as it a process that almost everyone is familiar with and relates to in one role or another. The objective of Incident Management is to restore and recover the service as quickly possible. Some of the CSF's for this to happen are:

- Ability to detect incidents as early as possible, possibly via monitoring tools
- Commitment from all staff to record all incidents into the service management tool. The quicker we know about it and get it to the right experts, the faster we can resolve it.
- Availability and accessibility of good quality information in the service management tool, as this also supports the support resource to resolve the issue as quickly as possible. The end user also has a vital role to play in this.
- Integration and availability of accurate and complete data in a CMDB so the resolver team can understand how this relates to other components and understand impact. For that matter, access to data like changes made to the service/CI's is also helpful.

The KPI's for Incident Management can be broken down into different sub-parts to better understand impact and performance in different areas:

KPI's for quality of incident resolution

- Percentage reduction in average time to respond to a call for assistance from first-line operatives.
- Percentage increase in the Incidents resolved by first line operatives.
- Percentage increase in the Incidents resolved by first line operatives on first responses
- Percentage reduction of Incidents incorrectly assigned.
- Percentage reduction of Incidents incorrectly categorized
- Percentage reduction in number of reopened Incidents.

Maintain IT service quality:

- Reduction in the service unavailability caused by Incidents
- Increased percentage of Incidents resolved within target times by priority and category.
- Percentage reduction in the average time for second line support to respond.
- Reduction of the Incident backlog.
- Percentage increase in the Incidents fixed before a user notices (e.g. via event management).
- Percentage reduction in the Incidents reopened
- Percentage reduction in the overall average time to resolve Incidents.
- Reduction in the number of Incidents requiring more than one second line support team.

Improve business and IT productivity:

- Percentage reduction in average cost of handling incidents
- Improve percentage of business incidents dealt with first line operatives
- Percentage reduction number of times first line operatives bypassed.
- Percentage improvement in average number of incidents handled by east first line operatives.
- No delays in the production of management reports
- Improved scores on satisfaction responses.

User satisfaction:

- Percentage improvement in satisfaction responses on the Incident resolution service.
- Percentage reduction in length of queue time waiting for Service Desk response.
- Percentage reduction in the number of lost service desk calls.
- Percentage reduction of the number of revised business instructions issued.

2.7 Self-service and SLA

As larger portions of externally sourced services move to the "as a service" delivery model, self-service becomes a huge component the delivery of the service. In fact, most organizations have been trying to promote end encourage self-service for many years anyway. There are of course challenges with the adoption of self-service as well as functionally and technically aggregating multiple suppliers' catalogues into one single usable portal. The retail space seems to have cracked this one though with large online marketplaces.

So if more and more things move to self-service, how do you define, agree, measure and deliver an SLA for self-service? There are of course ways and means to speed things up, but it does transfer a lot of the onus onto the end user for these to be achieved. Let's look at a non-IT example of checking in for a flight. Most frequent travelers now check in online using a self-service portal. Some low-cost airlines actually charge you extra if you check in at the airport, this is to push users to effectively self-serve as it reduces cost of resources required by the airline. Now, if you put your frequent flyer number while checking in, it will already have all your details and be a lot faster than if you had to input all the information from scratch. If people do not check in online, now they have even added kiosks at the airport for you to go and do it yourself, print your baggage tags and put them on yourself. So the SLA for quicker check in is actually entirely dependent on the end use. In enterprise IT, this can of course be done centrally by integrating your self-service portal with active directory or another LDAP service or even the HR system so that any information required on the user can be sought without the need for the user to input this.

My recommendation would be that every service offered has related requestable items published on a self-service portal. This is of benefit to the service provider, as well as provides a more consistent experience for end users. It will also reduce the processing time if the workflows for fulfillment are automated. Otherwise, users will effectively turn to assisted support. Another example is at a restaurant, if you opt for the buffet, you can go and get your food immediately or as per your convenience. Ala carte of course takes a lot longer. I agree that offering one or the other depends on the type of restaurant too. So there may be an industry, where the employees time is so valuable (lawyers who charge by the hour?) where you may not actually want them to spend any time on self-serving?

Back to the original question, could there be an SLA for self-service? The number of self-service components or requestable items as compared to the total number of services offered could be a good indicator. Number of issues resolved by the user using the knowledge base could be another.

2.8 Insanity in SLA (rise of unreason)

I am a worried at the decline of reason and the insurgence of unreason in our society in general and its proliferation into the business world as well. It has enormous implications on resolutions of any problem. This trend has not emerged abruptly but developed slowly over a period of time. One of the primary catalysts for the rise of unreason is people's appetite for junk opinion (just like junk food). Unfortunately, technology has fueled it by making it easily to quickly propagate bad information to a very large audience and very easy for users to consume. You can propagate an opinion from anywhere to anyone at any time; thanks to mobility and a connected world (Facebook, Twitter, WhatsApp etc.).

In the past, especially during the pre-web era, opinions were formed with depth and thoroughness of the facts and largely established through books and periodicals including newspapers' opinion columns. Corresponding to that we had information technology magazines that would establish an opinion based on details. With the proliferation of the web, books and white papers were diluted by blogs and in the past few years it is further diluted by tweets. **Depth** is a rare thing of the past.

We are now firmly in an era of immature opinions where substance is not the logic, reason and thinking behind the opinion, but the weightage that is acquired by rallying around the opinion tweets. Twitter has oversimplified the trading of opinions where depth is hidden or even non-existent. Substance is the numbers game.

This trend is reflected in IT as well in the form of immature software products where the substance or value is not in the product as such, but in the weightage, it acquires by getting customers rallying around it. Making a good product is not as important as developing a strong logic/algorithm, but rather a matter of building a customer base, regardless of the quality or value. It can be argued that a customer can be rallied on the basis of merit of the product but that is not necessary. It can be done by alternate skills of marketing or even buying the customer base with vested interests. This phenomenon resonates with the phenomenon of artificial stupidity that I discussed in my first book – *"Process Excellence for IT Operations"*. Rather than educating people on how to create an informed opinion, we teach people what opinion to make.

With SLAs, we create ones that can't be measured (several examples so far in this book), ones that add no value and others that are simply unrealistic. If you do not invest in, change your architecture and technology you use to develop and deliver services, you cannot realistically expect to achieve higher SLAs or availability or quality of service. The expectation is that by outsourcing to another vendor at a cheaper price will make things better.

There is also ambiguity in several SLAs; my favorite is FCR. *Is it first contact or first call?* I have seen both being used. Does it include only issues that are resolvable at the desk or all? If all, have you actually given the service desk the authority and access required for all systems to be able to resolve tickets? What if the provider puts in automated tools to handle issues and requests, case in point being password reset tools. If a user then uses this tool to resolve their issue, does that count towards the FCR? If not, what is the incentive for the supplier to automate it, when it is so easy to add to your FCR performance by manually resetting the password when the user calls the desk? So we not only ambiguity, we also have misconceptions by design. Another one is availability. If the entire service is down, it is easy to calculate. It is black and white or up and down. But what if the service is unavailable to one of 10 locations, is that 10% unavailability? What if that one location houses 80% of the user base? How is that factored in? Every supplier proposes what works best for them and over a period of time, the confusion and interpretation of best practice gets even more muddy.

The following example defines different business hours for various days of the week and ticket priority. Needless to say that it complicates the SLA calculation, but can be essential for business requirement.

Support Hours by Priority	**Workdays**	**Saturdays**	**Sundays**	**Public Holidays**
Priority 1	24/7	24/7	24/7	24/7
Priority 2	07:00 to 23:00	08:00 to 18:00	12:00 to 20:00	12:00 to 20:00
Priority 3	07:00 to 23:00	08:00 to 18:00	N/A	N/A
Priority 4	07:00 to 17:00	N/A	N/A	N/A

The following example shows the defined SLA for incident tickets of different priorities. In addition to determining whether the vendor achieved the SLA, they apply a penalty by determining how much time elapsed after the SLA milestone was missed.

Performance Indicator	**Small Service Level Deviation**	**Major Service Level Deviation**	**Critical Service Level Deviation**
Time to restore Incidents Category A	N/A	>2 hours up to 4 hours	> 4-6 hrs (+one additional CSLD for each additional started hour)
Time to restore Incidents Category B	>2 hours up to 4 hours	>4 hours up to 6 hours	> 6-10 hrs (+one additional CSLD for each additional started 2nd hour)
Time to restore Incidents Category C	> 2 days up to 5 days	> 5 days (+one additional MSLD for each additional started 2nd day)	N/A
Time to restore Incidents Category D	Not resolved and accepted in time for agreed release	N/A	N/A

The following are few examples of SLA definitions which are either inherently baseless or incorrect. Some sound very simple, but will be quite difficult to calculate objectively and even if we do calculate them, what do we achieve?

SLA definition	Comment
Percentage incident registration in the ITSM tool	It is not even possible to calculate the defined metric.
Number of milestones achieved according to problem solution path	It is subjective to attempt to calculate this SLA
All problems should be resolved within a reasonable timeframe	How do you measure this SLA or define what is reasonable?
The percentage of accuracy on the CMDB and its availability for Customer	An old classic, but very subjective
Backup restoration time	The backup restoration time depends on the amount of data being restored. All backups cannot be completed within 2 hours
Percentage of requests solved in 1st line (by Service Desk)	Again an old classic, but very subjective to define and calculate
Time to route Incident Category A and B correctly to either SI or Workplace Services Vendor	This SLA would be very difficult to calculate as automation will be extremely difficult.
Service Order Delivery Precision	I don't know what this even means

Why is there this rise of unreason? Is it purely because our lives are busy and chaotic at the moment that we do not have the time to pause and thing? Or is that we do not prioritize the right things and all of our time is consumed elsewhere? Or is it that we just do not have the motivation anymore? We are conditioned by instant gratification. So with the rise of unreason all around us, why should SLAs be left behind?

Knowledge is growing, but wisdom is not

A lot of data is being produced every single day. We now even have a term for it – "big *data*". And other have capitalized on this with software products to sift through the garbage. There are analytics tools for making any sense of this huge amount of data, effectively turning it into information. Turning that *information* into knowledge is a lot harder, as it depends on the individual. So how do we get to wisdom? If you applied artificial intelligence technology or machine learning capabilities on knowledge, would it be *wisdom*. Answer is not necessarily yes. It is just using technology to make sense of information and *knowledge* and act upon it, instead of a human. Yes, it can do it lot faster. So where does wisdom come in, as it depends on the intent and the purpose. Wisdom has a grander scope and a positive purpose is attached to it. Data, information and knowledge is a "fact", enabled by technology. Wisdom is the "truth", which technology cannot always help with.

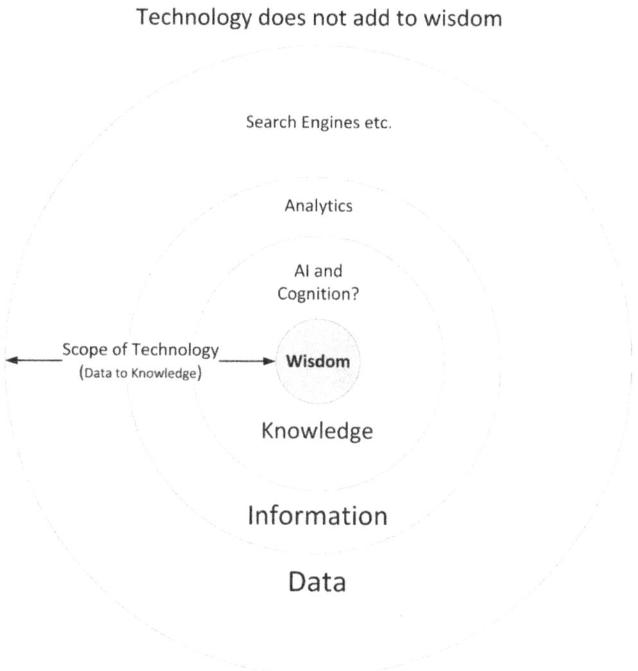

Figure 16: Data to wisdom

Data is discrete, objective facts about an event. It can be quantitatively measured by cost, speed and capacity. The qualitative measures are timeliness, relevance and clarity.
Information is a message meant to change receiver's perception. It can be quantitatively measured by connectivity and transaction. The qualitative measures are informativeness and usefulness.
Knowledge is experience, values, context applied to a message. It can be quantitatively measured by contextual and evaluative attribute. The qualitative measures are intuitive and informative.
Wisdom is collective application of knowledge that provides expertise and capability in the multiple tenets such as experience, grounded truth, judgments, values and beliefs. In shortest term, wisdom is the matter of using knowledge with sense of responsibility for positive purpose and sense of humanity.

And we have the same issue with wisdom and knowledge! We also seem to be getting dumber by the day, requiring technology to solve the most basic of reasoning. People look at the temperature, wind, humidity to decide if they should be feeling "hot or cold", you don't need that, your body tells you if you feel hot to feel cold. The reality is there is a real lack of wisdom. The space is just too crowded with data and some information. Twitter for example is just one source of data and opinions. Every second, on average, around 6,000 tweets are tweeted on Twitter, which corresponds to over 350,000 tweets sent per minute, 500 million tweets per day and around 200 billion tweets per year. To put the amount of wisdom into context, let's look at the solar system *(source for facts and figures: Wikipedia https://en.wikipedia.org/wiki/Solar_System).*

The Solar System is the gravitationally bound system comprising the Sun and the objects that orbit it, either directly or indirectly. Of those objects that orbit the Sun directly, the largest eight are the planets, with the remainder being smaller objects, such as dwarf planets and small Solar System bodies. The asteroid belt, which lies between the orbits of Mars and Jupiter, mostly contains objects composed, like the terrestrial planets, of rock and metal. Beyond Neptune's orbit lie the Kuiper belt and scattered disc. The distance from the sun to the Kuiper cliff is 50 AU or astronomical unit. One astronomical unit is roughly the distance from Earth to the Sun, which is 150 million kilometers or 93 million miles. The sun's gravitational pull is felt 50 AUs away, or 7.5 billion kilometers away! The Sun's mass is about 330,000 times that of earth, but more shockingly, it makes up 99.86% of the total mass of the Solar System. It is same thing with wisdom (inversely), of which there is very little and probably makes up 0.14% of all of the knowledge that exists! It looks like our world of data; information knowledge and wisdom is a manifestation of nature itself and nature is supreme!

We have similar contradictions and issues in other areas of our world too:

- Truth vs fact *(and now thanks to US politics, we have new term called alternate facts too!).* Truth is a generally accepted outcome or reasoning while fact is a proven truth, in other words every fact is true but not all truths are facts. Example 2+2=4 is a fact (there can only be one result so it is a proven truth).
- Thinking vs reasoning: Thinking is a broad term, generally referring to all conscious activity of the mind. Reasoning is a particular type, mode, category, or kind of thought, specifically and intentionally focused on logical problem solving or rational thought. Do we need to think to reason? Most reasoning today are not based on any thinking.
- Accountability vs responsibility: we have already discussed these terms earlier in the book, but this so often mixed up and confused.
- Freedom vs liberty: Freedom carries the sense of responsibility and therefore has some boundary while the liberty has no boundary. Freedom is usually granted while liberty is taken.

3 How to develop sensible SLA

In section *2.1 What is a SLA?* we explained in detail, what an SLA is and what it does. A picturized summary of that section provides our SLA development approach as depicted below.

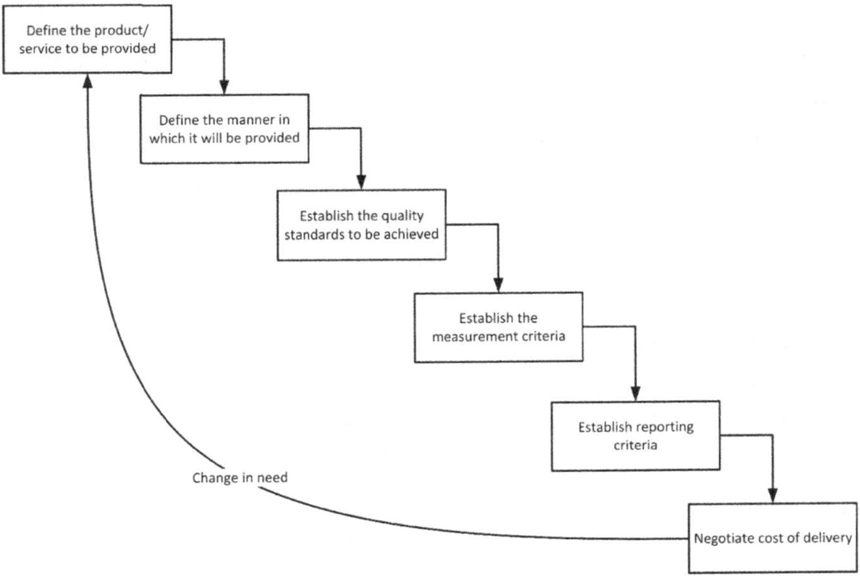

Figure 17: SLA Development Approach

Subsequent sections provide detailed guidance on top of the approach and will be clearer as you go through the concept of the SLA architecture.

It is also important to draw a balance between coverage of services and number of KPI's and SLAs for each. See figure below:

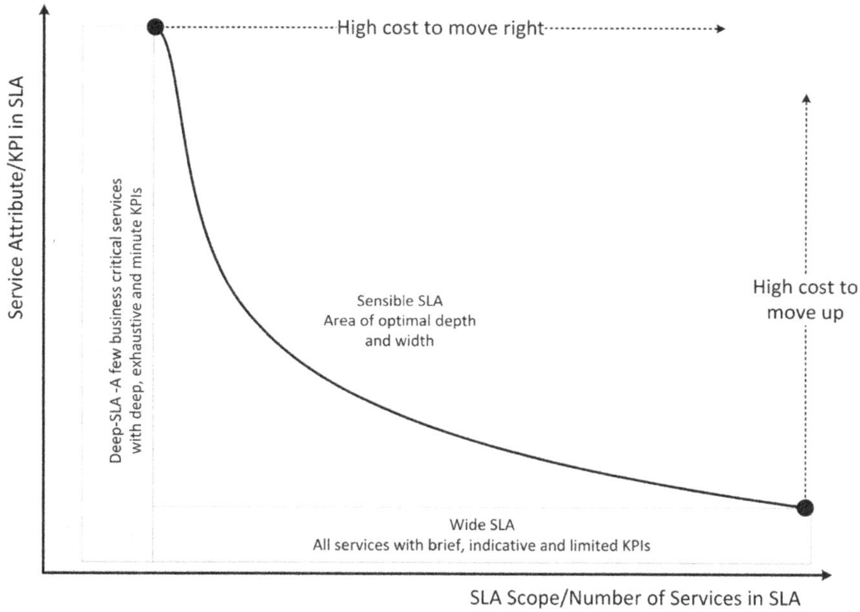

Figure 18: "Deep and Wide" SLAs

3.1 Introducing the concept of SLA architecture

In Hindu philosophy, there is a belief that God exists in every living thing and a pious person sees God in everything. Similarly, in the role of an architect, I see Architecture in everything I deal with. *Architecture* as a discipline that originated from civil engineering centuries ago and is defined as the art or practice of designing and constructing buildings. Later this term was generalized and defined as the complex or carefully designed structure of something and went beyond buildings or civil

In IT, initially it was applied to computers and then further expanded in the area of network, applications and software in general as specifying the overall structure, logical components, and the logical interrelationships of a computer, its operating system, a network and application. An architecture can be a reference model, such as the Open Systems Interconnection (OSI) reference model that includes every layer, from hardware to the user interface part of the software or it can be a specific product architecture, such as that for manufacturer specific CPU (Intel Xeon for example) or for a manufacturer specific operating system (IBM OS/400 for example).

It is common for the term architecture to be interchangeably used with design, but design has a lesser scope than architecture. Architecture is a design, but every design is not architecture. A single component or a new function has a design that has to fit within the overall architecture (for example individual component designs in client server architecture). A similar term, framework, can be thought of as the structural part of an architecture. In service management area ITIL, IT4IT and COBIT are examples of the frameworks upon which each organization is architecting its service management systems. Architecture is influenced by the organization (customers and users), technical environment and even the architect's experience.

Have you heard of SLA architecture? I am certain you haven't, and neither have I, because I am introducing this concept. All of us have are familiar with other types architecture including business architecture; we know what architecture is and why it is necessary to build and manage any tangible object. We introduced service management architecture and service architecture in our earlier books and are now introducing SLA architecture. SLA architecture will, like any other architecture, specify the overall structure, logical components, and the logical interrelationships among those components defined in an SLA.

IT Managers have unknowingly complied with this architecture in most of the SLAs.

3.1.1 Service Architecture

Our traditional definition of a service holds good as that is the very fundamental that will never change – A Service is a set of benefits realized by the execution of a set of activities by a function (person(s)) or by machine(s) (configuration item(s)) or by both. Therefore the set of activities will form the core of our service architecture, however, surrounding the set of service producing CIs forming the service map/physical model of service the logical and conceptual model of a service describing service properties and realized by the data model will actually be the holistic service architecture.

Service architecture defines the nine key elements of service properties surrounding the composition of the service.

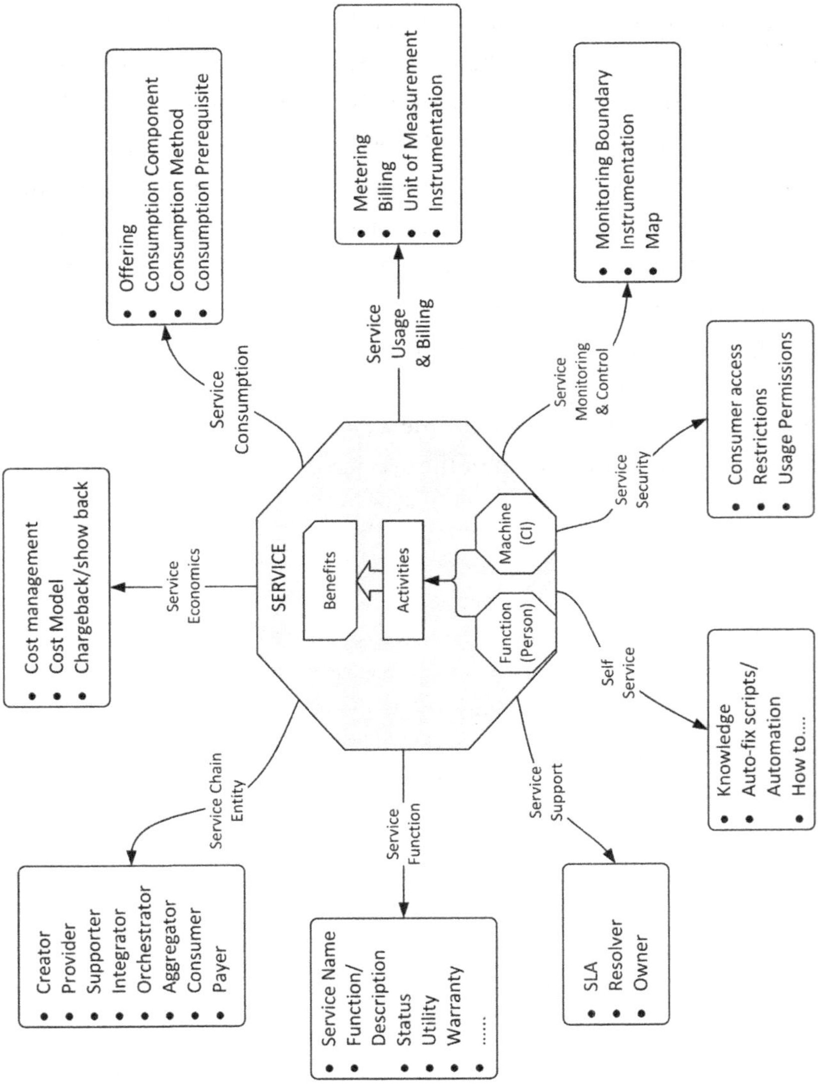

Figure 19: Service Architecture

So how do we differentiate between the different, but inter related architectures?

- Service Management architecture: focuses on the design and lifecycle management of processes, associated tools and functions
- Service architecture: focuses on the design and management of components of a service
- SLA architecture focuses on the design and management of the SLA of services. A barometer to gauge the accuracy of the SLA is that the service is running as designed and can be measured correctly.

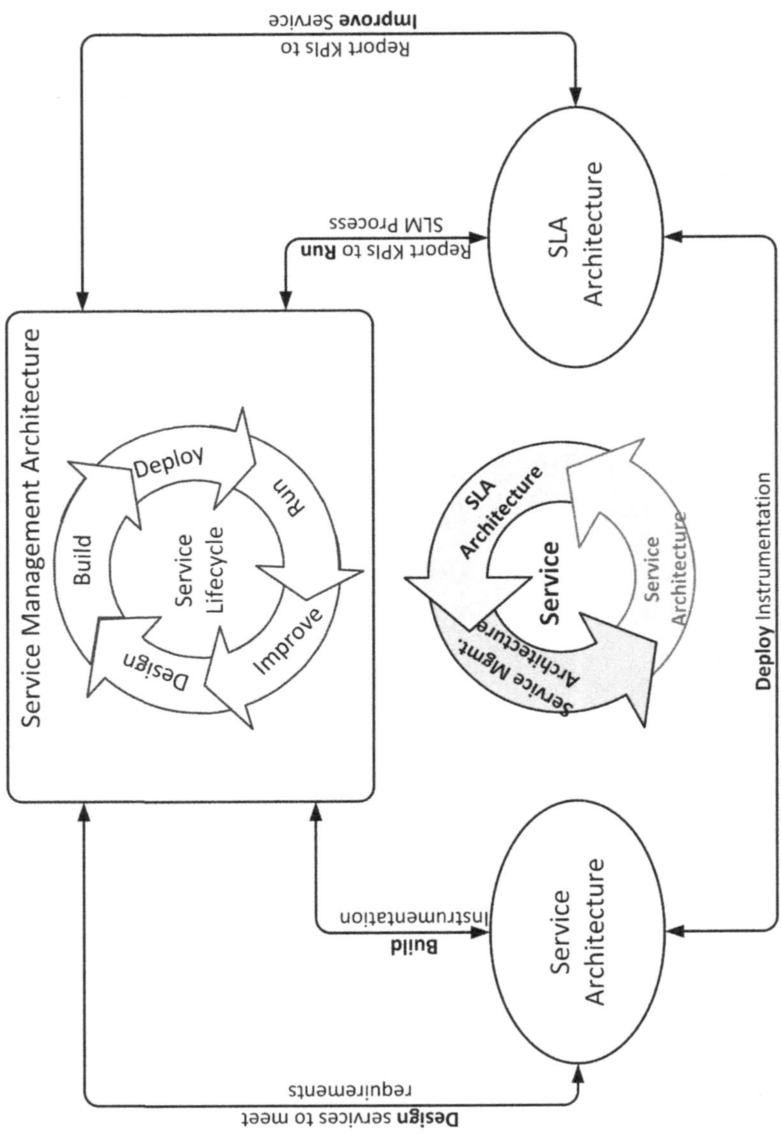

Figure 20: Service Management, Service & SLA Architecture

Service architecture also becomes important when you think beyond technology and of business services. Also think of the digital world, where IT is the mainstream business, not an enabler. XaaS would be the de facto business model, and service architecture would be critical.

Service management architecture vs service architecture vs SLA architecture

Service Management Architecture

- Helps to manage the service lifecycle from strategy to operation
- Depicts the interconnection of entire service management system that includes processes, underlying technologies (systems and tools), and functions

Service Architecture

- Part of toolkit in service strategy phase of service management lifecycle
- Helps to design the service for consumption purposes
- Depicts the different elements/components of a service and relationship

SLA Architecture

- Helps to design the service SLA that sets the expectation of the customer as well as provides criteria to measure performance
- Depicts the different elements of an SLA and relationship to other components of the services

The above three are in a hierarchy and related, but independent of each other. This book references and provides guidance on the SLA architecture.

3.1.2 SLA Architecture

The SLA architecture represents the different elements of an SLA and how they connect to each other.

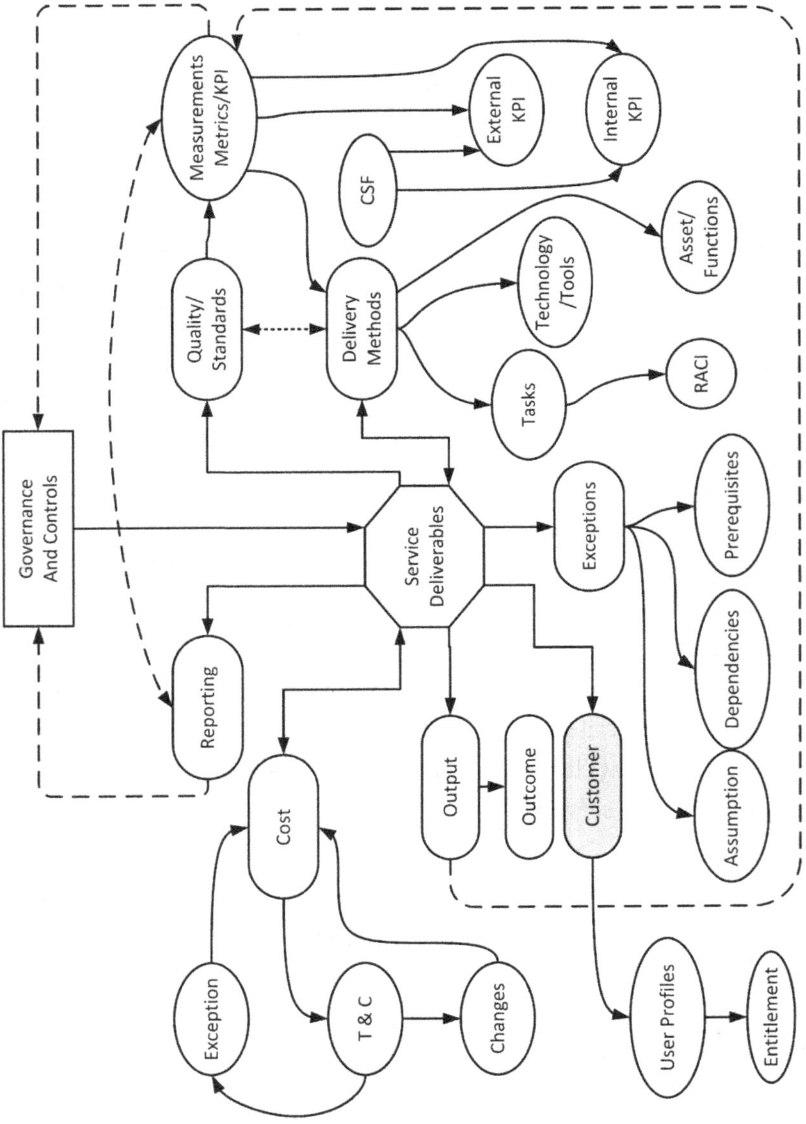

Figure 21: SLA Architecture

1. Customer; this can also include a VIP customer that receives an elevated level of service as compared to standard users. A user's profile and entitlement will dictate if they are authorized to consume the service. The term customer here relates to both the folks paying for the service and consumers using the service.
2. Cost: this is the definition and listing of what the service will deliver and at what cost. Remember the old saying - *if you pay peanuts, you will get monkeys.* Changing the cost of the service will have a direct impact to the ability of delivering the service deliverables at the agreed SLA. The two-sided arrow suggests that in real life the origination or amendment of SLAs may be triggered by cost revisions.
3. Quality and standard – Service deliverables are governed by or required to comply with the quality and standards and should be measurable against those criteria. The quality is dependent upon human factors on both the sides and can rarely be delivered in exactly the same way repeatedly because at the core of this is the moment of interaction between humans. Even if the service could be delivered repeatedly in exactly the same manner, the perception of quality will differ because each customer's perception would not be the same. Based on experience, it is nearly impossible to maintain the consistent service quality in large scale of service support operation due to the human element, at the same time, the customer also influences the quality that he deserves to get. Internal and external KPI's will be related to this to measure the performance and quality.
4. Delivery Method – Service deliverables and delivery method impact each other. Delivery method is very critical as it has a relationship with deliverables, measurements/KPIs, and quality. The delivery method dictates the tasks to be performed, technology and tools to be used and asset and people involved. The task indirectly dictates the RACI.
5. Exceptions (things that are out of scope) will also cover assumptions, dependencies and pre-requisites.
6. Output – deliverables will produce an output, which will further support an outcome. The outcome is the result, the consequence, the difference made by deliverables and the benefits realized.

7. Reporting of the service deliverables and the agreed measurements and KPIs
8. Governance and control: Governance is not management/executive oversight, that is a common misconception. Governance is a highly misused term and often just provides oversight. If you need to change this to oversight, then by design your goal of governance is failing. Governance is a method of assurance that the right decision will be taken by the right person. This is the only goal of governance; how this is done is by ensuring the quorum are made up of the right attendees, at the required frequency, with access to the required information and ensuring that the right folks are empowered to make decisions.

3.1.3 Legal aspects of SLA

You cannot solve technology problems with legal tools. Unfortunately, a lot of contracts are written in such way, so as to try and penalize the supplier if things go wrong, which they will invariably do if the underlying architecture doesn't exist to support delivery of the service. In an IT outsourcing deal, the SME's, architects and operations manager should be the focal point, sadly in many of them, it is instead the legal team, while operations is pushed into the background. There is no argument that there should be a legal contract and recourse, but overwhelmingly changing a service management affair to a legal affair is incorrect.

Agreement vs contract

Many people use the terms "contract" and "agreement" interchangeably, but they are not precisely the same thing. An agreement is any understanding or arrangement reached between service provider and customer. A contract is a specific type of agreement that, by its terms and elements, is legally binding and enforceable in a court of law, therefore, a contract has more rigidly documented term than those in an agreement.

Purpose of legal parts in SLA (the legal contract)

The irony- You need to and possibly want to trust the service provider you are doing business with, but don't trust him too much! Sometimes you need to remember why you engaged with the supplier. There are of course aspects of the service that need to be described, worded as such to be backed up by local laws. It is after all a contractual and professional relationship and the legal aspects are necessary to protect both the supplier and the client. The optimal points to address in a legal contract are:

1. Price - What is included, excluded and optional
2. Payment terms – within x number of days of invoicing, in advance or arrears, etc.
3. Duration – start date and end dates
4. Changes to the service and how they are to be costed
5. Upgrade rights and eligibility
6. Support hours
7. Licensing model
8. Warranty clause
9. Termination
10. Indemnification
11. Arbitration

Why the overwhelming legal language?

We have already agreed that legal protection is required by both parties. But the moment technical and legal professionals collaborate to develop the legal contract; a variety of jargon starts surfacing. It happens in the technology world all the time but during the contract development, legal jargon take front and center seat. I was under the impression that the IT industry invents and manufactures buzzwords and jargon in bulk, but I have come across similar trends in other businesses too, though the IT industry is still far ahead of the pack. The IT industry is a game of manufacturing and playing with buzzwords. Some real high value and sensible ideas are created outside the IT industry like Lean, but folks bring it into the IT world, start adapting it and drift in a totally different direction. Lean is about elimination of wasteful or non-value-add work and thus improving efficiency. Agility is about minimizing the inertia to achieve speed by reducing quantum of work within a specific time duration. But heavy use of these jargons has given rise to individual interpretations. Jargons mask the real meaning and serve the vested interest of a few stakeholders who use it to hide the failure of unclear thinking, but not serve the business interest of the organizations entering into the contract. Avoidance of jargons require hard work (thinking hard is hard work indeed) and not easy to do. Jargons provide an easy way out. The other issue I have seen is getting SMEs to input into contracts. The statement I hear is "delivery needs to review, redline and sign it off". Fair enough. That is a need to validate that what is being committed can and will be delivered by the folks who are responsible for it. But, SMEs are not lawyers. Certain words have a specific meaning in law. "Best endeavor" vs "reasonable endeavor". Best implies that whatever is theoretically possible. So if you had to fly a resource half way around the world to provide support, then you would need to do it. But that isn't reasonable or cost effective.

Attempt to solve technical problem with legal tools?

In the IT industry, tool vendors promise to solve process problem with tools similarly legal professionals promise to solve technology problem with legal tools like SLA contract terms. The focus is shifted to meet the agreement rather than the spirit of the agreement and the loser is the actual service users. e.g. Rhetorical distinction between the terminologies without the difference in the meaning – extremely careless act is not prosecutable, but a grossly negligent act is.

Let me give you an example of trying to use a legal tool to solve a technical problem. There was a large IT outsourcing company that focused solely on the healthcare services industry. The set out to create a huge centralized database that would hold all patient data, which would be provided by healthcare providers. Each provider could then access only their own data. But the reality was, there weren't sufficient security controls to guarantee access controls. There was a possibility that a provider may be able to see patient records provided by another provider. When the firm was asked "what happens if customer A accessed the data of customer B?", they replied "oh, customer A won't do that, because we have a clause in the contract that the won't access any other data apart from their own. If they do and we get sued by the customer B whose data was exposed, we will in turn sue customer A for breach of contract". So this is a classic case of using a legal tool, to solve a technical need (security, data separation and access control). The outcome is the same I guess.

3.2 SLA Development principles

Some general principles to follow when designing SLAs

- *Separate SLAs for each IT service*

  Avoid creating broad ranging SLAs that apply to all services, as it may not be required, will make measuring more complex and will more than likely not meet business needs. For example, for service requests, avoid basing them on a priority and making them generic, providing a laptop will take longer than creating a user account. Be specific for each service. Some may also require approvals due to a commercial impact, factor those aspects into your SLA (e.g. SLA clock only starts after all approvals are provided).
- *SLA for a purpose*

  Each SLA must serve a purpose and parameter. You should be able to clearly articulate what the purpose is and what insight is it providing. The payroll process runs twice a month, so they only become critical at a point in time. However, a standard availability SLA is tied across the board for all services or infrastructure (99.9% availability).
- *Measure the SLA only on system generated timestamps*

Anything that can be manually input will be eventually manipulated to meet the criteria.

- *An SLA must be quantitative and achievable*
  An SLA measurement should not be a number picked from the air, nor a compromise in a negotiation with the customer. SLAs should be based on quantitative data and be realistic and achievable. An SLA should reflect the suppliers experience and expertise with a clear understanding of what it takes to deliver the service based on the environment, skills, resources and technology – both the clients and the suppliers, along with testing and prototyping the service during the design and continual improvement phases. An SLA for how long it should take to install a patch for example, should be an actual, achievable number that the service provider is capable of achieving based on the resources available.
- SLAs must be measurable
  If you cannot measure it, then you cannot manage it. We have already seen some examples of SLAs that just cannot be measured, they serve no purpose.
- SLAs must be aligned to requirements
  In contracts and SLAs there is a tendency to mention what is possible, rather than what is required. The SLA must be directly related to the IT service being delivered and it must be relevant to evaluating performance against that goal
- SLAs require periodic review and adjustment
  SLAs should be reviewed to ensure they are still fit for purpose and updated whenever there are any proposed changes that affect service hours, availability, uptime, completion, or response time.

There are multiple approaches that can be taken when designing SLAs. Either the service is designed to meet required SLAs or the best SLAs can be offered based on the designed service. For example, the American approach to car design – set a price point – then work backwards to work out what was the best quality that could be given at that price. The European approach to car design was very different, set the quality standards –then work backward on how to deliver that at the lowest price.

3.2.1 Complexity vs purposefulness of SLA

Why more can be less

In *Figure 22: Complexity versus Purposefulness of SLA* below, complexity refers to the difficulty of description and the difficulty of interpretation of SLA parameters and measurement formulae and purpose refer to the value for the customer.

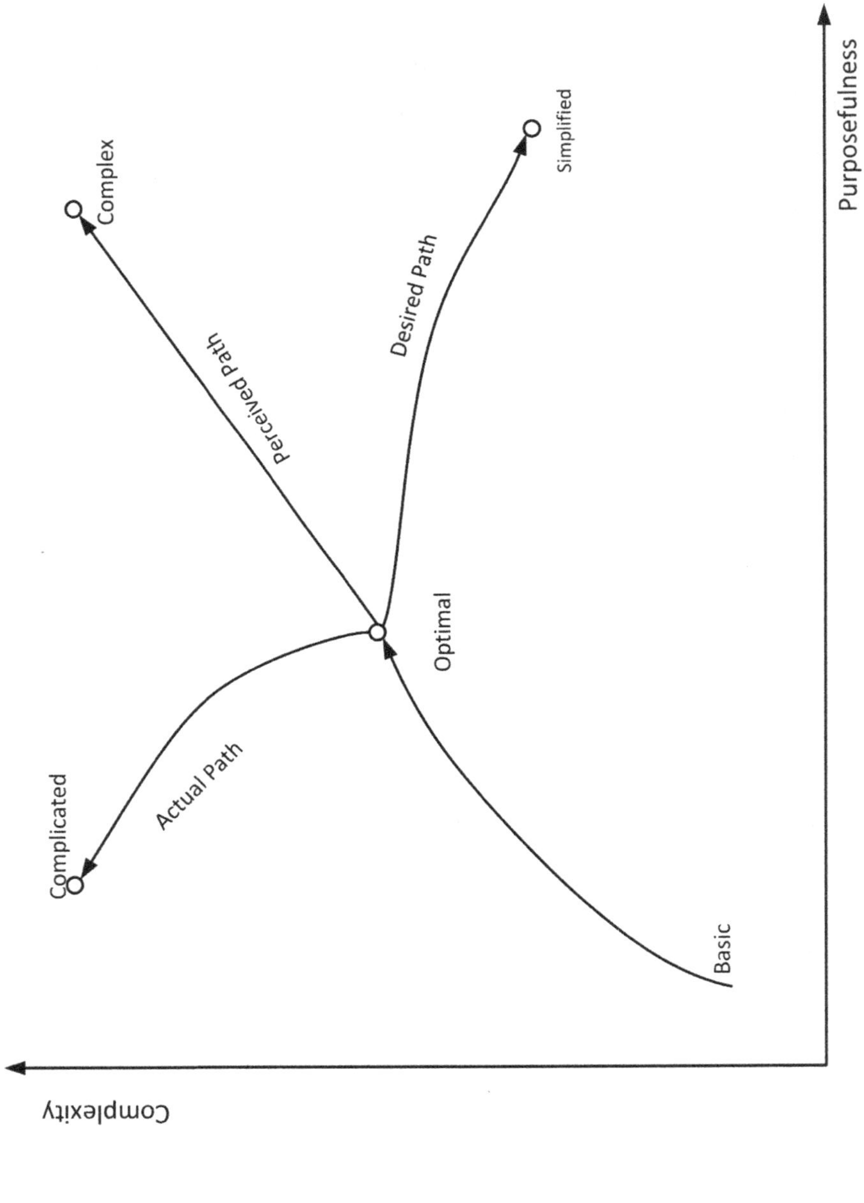

Figure 22: Complexity versus Purposefulness of SLA

Complexity for a purpose: Airline example

Airline industry is extremely mature in establishing a complex but successful model for delivering variable service levels to its customers. It is successful because it serves the business purpose extremely well. The complexity is hidden from customers, but they fully understand the outcome and the relation between the service level and the price.
Most people do not understand the difference between the fare class and cabin class. Most of the airlines offer three cabin classes *(United airline for example names them as Global First, Business First, First and Economy).* Most airplanes have two class cabins. In economy cabin, there is further division - Economy and Economy Plus. However, the fares classes are many. For example, United has as many as 39 fare classes. United uses these classes to determine the level of the services and benefits and perks to the passenger not only during travel but beyond it as well. Actually, the service level during the travel period are one to four depending upon the type of airplane but each of these 39 fare classes translate into different levels of perks and benefits from check in to baggage delivery at the end of the travel and status in the loyalty program.

A customer also has multiple status level as defined by the loyalty program of the airline. The service level (and indirectly the service quality) is a combination of:

1. The cabin class
2. The fare class
3. The passenger status

Purposefulness and complexity are not always directly proportional. It is easy to make things complex (leading to complicated) and also reduce the purpose. We have seen some example SLAs in IT that are extremely complex and serve little purpose in *section 2.8 - Insanity in SLA (Rise of Unreason).* Starting at "basic" may not sufficient, but a starting point. The intention should then be to increase the SLAs and metrics by providing better insights into performance, therefore the purposefulness, but not the complexity. If you can get to an "optimal" state, you would have reached a point of workable SLAs. As you then add new parameters related to quality and standards, the measurement methodology should be simplified to follow the "desired path", but the reality is that most organizations end up complicating it.

All transaction-based services (e.g. incident management, request fulfilment), it is common to define a response time and the resolution/fulfilment time. For perpetual services the availability and performance SLAs are common. Performance may be non-measurable and can be expressed in subjective worlds like "reasonably acceptable".

Complex SLA

Purposefulness should increase, and simplification should be done – leading down the desired path. Many a time, you may want to increase the purposefulness and believe that complexity will increase linearly and that is ok, this will take you down the perceived path. In several cases, you make it complicated and the purposefulness suffers – this will take you down the actual path

Complexity versus complicatedness

Complex is different to complicated. Complexity is often essential in the modern world, but complication is the negative part of the complexity. Complicatedness is the unnecessary complexity and occurs when non-value-added parameters are added in the SLA

- Complexity is natural progression, complication is enforced
- Legal teams play a very good role in making it complicated

Resource Unit Complexity

A resource unit is a chargeable component. It could a lower level detail of the catalog of services that you offer. Below is an example of a resource unit sheet from one client, you can only imagine the overhead of measuring and reporting on this:

Tower - Data Center	
AS400 Servers - Tier 1 - mission critical images Physical	Count of LPARs
AS400 Servers - Tier 2 - production images Physical	Count of LPARs
Mainframe Processing Mainframe	MIPS
Linux Svr - Mission Critical - Standard Service	Count of OSI
Linux Svr - Non-Mission Critical - Standard Service	Count of OSI
Linux Svr - Tier 1 - Mission Critical Images Physical Provisioned	Count of OSI
Linux Svr - Tier 2 - Production Image Physical Provisioned	Count of OSI
Linux Svr - Tier 2 - Production Images Virtual - Provisioned	Count of OSI
Linux Svr - Tier 3 - Dev/Test Image Physical Provisioned	Count of OSI
Linux Svr - Tier 3 - Dev/Test Image Virtual - Provisioned	Count of OSI

Linux Svr - Tier 3 - Dev/Test Image Physical Provisioned	Count of OSI
Linux Svr - Tier 3 - Dev/Test Image Virtual - Provisioned	Count of OSI
Wintel Svr - Mission Critical - Standard Service	Count of OSI
Wintel Svr - Non-Mission Critical - Standard Service	Count of OSI
Wintel Svr - Tier 1 - Mission Critical Image Physical Provisioned	Count of OSI
Wintel Svr - Tier 1 - Mission Critical Image Virtual Provisioned	Count of OSI
Wintel Svr - Tier 2 - Production Image Physical Provisioned	Count of OSI
Wintel Svr - Tier 2 - Production Image Virtual Provisioned	Count of OSI
Wintel Svr - Tier 3 - Dev/Test Image Physical Provisioned	Count of OSI
Wintel Svr - Tier 3 - Dev/Test Image Virtual Provisioned	Count of OSI
HPUX - Non Prod	Count of OSI
HPUX - Prod	Count of OSI
SAP Ignite Servers	Count of OSI
SAP Retail Servers	Count of OSI

SAP X86 Servers	Count of OSI
SAN Storage - Tier 1 - Standard Service	GB
SAN Storage - Tier 2 - Standard Service	GB
SAN Storage - Tier 3 - Standard Service	GB
SAN Storage - Tier 1 - Provisioned	GB
SAN Storage - Tier 2 - Provisioned	GB
SAN Storage - Tier 3 - Provisioned	GB
Backup Data - Provisioned	GB
Backup Data	GB
Archival	GB
Storage Standard Service	GB
Database - Informix	Count of instances
Database - Oracle	Count of instances
Database - SQL Server	Count of databases
Database - Neteeza	Count of databases
Mailbox	Count of mailboxes
SharePoint	Count of sites
Secure File Transfer Program (SFTP) License	Count of instances

SecureAuth	Count of desktop /laptop users
Tower - Cloud	
Azure - Dev/Test Virtual	Count of OSI
Azure - Mission Critical Virtual	Count of OSI
Azure - Production Virtual	Count of OSI
Azure Backup Comvault	GB
Azure Backup Master Server	Count of OSI
Azure Backup Media Server	Count of OSI
Tower - Network	
Data Network Data Ports (DC Switch)	Count of total ports
Data Network Data Ports (Field Switch) Provisioned	Count of active ports
Data Network Data Ports (Field Switch) Standard Service	Count of active ports
Gigamon Network TAP	Count of sites
Loadbalancer - Provisioned	Count of devices
Loadbalancer	Count of devices
Routers	Count of devices
VPN Router - Provisioned	Count of devices

Unified Communication - Voice Support - Provisioned	Count of UC users
Unified Communication - Voice Support	Count of UC users
Wireless Access Points & Wireless Lan Controllers - Provisioned	Count of devices
Wireless Access Points & Wireless Lan Controllers	Count of devices
Voice Network - PBX - Voice	Count of end point

Complexity of definition vs the complexity of measurement

The IT industry enjoys obfuscation. Obfuscation is the practice of making something difficult to understand. It was deliberately adopted in application programming where code is often obfuscated to protect intellectual property and prevent an attacker from reverse engineering a proprietary software program. There are different levels and forms of obfuscation, such as encrypting some or all of the code, renaming useful class and variable names to meaningless labels or adding unused or meaningless code to an application binary. It is so important and necessary that even obfuscator tools are available to automatically convert simple and straight source code into a program that works the same way, but is much harder to read and understand.

SLA Datapoints

Your process should be designed to generate the data points for the SLA. You may agree an SLA which may require your processes to be reengineered. E.g. when you outsource a service and insist that the supplier uses your ITSM tool. They will be governed by the same processes that were

ITSM tool. They will be governed by the same processes that were designed to be delivered by internal teams and do not support an external supplier to align to them and still meet their contractually agreed SLAs.

3.2.2 Defining the utility and warranty of service

While we often think of a "utility" as an item or service that we use (like gas or electricity), the concept is actually derived from an economic concept that utility is "is it fit for purpose" and meant to do. So some of the utility parameters of a service would be:

- Meeting customer need
- What does it do?
- Functionality

if we were to look at an example of an e-mail service, then the utility criteria would be:

- Can send and receive e-mail
- Send and receive attachment
- Access via internet from anywhere
- Use on any device

Warranty on the other hand is a promise that a product or service is "Fit for Use." Some of the criteria of warranty would be:

- Available when you need -free from outage
- Performance acceptable – (download time for example)
- Secure – protected from unauthorized access

3.2.3 Service Quality and SLA

A Service is interaction and exchange between two parties: namely, the service receiver and service provider. Therefore, the service quality should be solely influenced by the actions and exchanges between these two parties. However, in service quality gaps, you will notice the influence of third parties that have no business in the service transactions also impacts the service quality and introduces the gaps. This influence is because of direct and indirect communication about the services that sets the customer's expectations. For example, I heard great things about a long-distance phone-service provider from my friend and opted to go for it. I was not satisfied because my expectations were set by my friend, who was not an authorized promise-maker for the service provider. The brand value of the provider also provokes some buyer expectations.

The gap really starts with the contractual statement of work (SOW) at the foundation. SOW may not truly reflect the expectations of the customer, and also SOW may not provide the expectation parameters to the service provider, leaving these parameters open for interpretation. Since SOW drives the service provider's perception of expected service, deficiency on the SOW on the expected service sets the foundation of further gaps. Many times, the service provider prepares to deliver extraordinary things and delivers them "ordinarily," and the customer is still not excited because the end result is ordinary. Service providers may miss the point that the customer is expecting ordinary things but "extraordinary" delivery. I have seen SOW describing the implementation of a financial-management process for IT service. While the service provider thought of implementation cost models and the charge-back system, the customer was expecting "timely submission of error-free invoices" as the outcome. The SOW design approach is for contract arbitration rather than for relationship-building, and this is one of the weaknesses in operation.

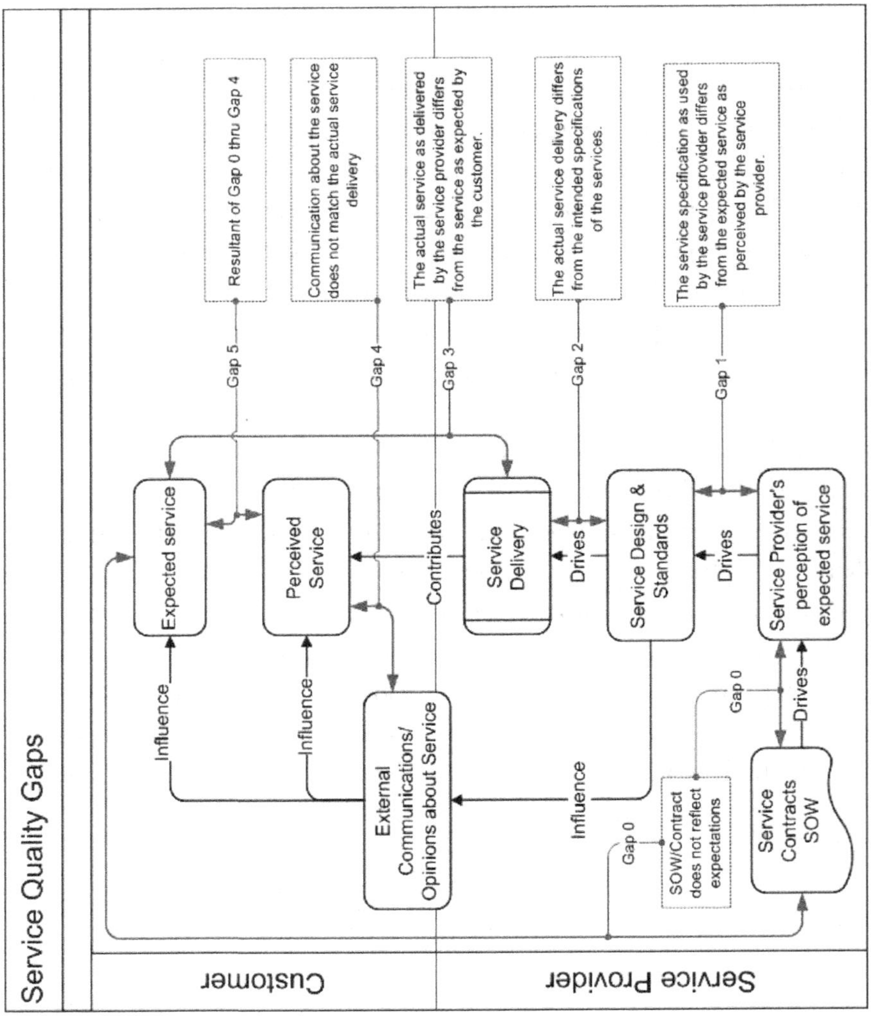

Figure 23: Service quality gap model

An important point to note here is that the customer is an equal partner in setting the foundation of the gap. This has referred as Gap 0 in the diagram above.
Once SOW is finalized, a service provider develops the standards and sets the service delivery systems (people, process, tools, etc.) based on those standards. Many times, the standards are already defined and accounted for while developing the SOW. The service provider thinks that the standards to design the service are based on the SOW and therefore will deliver the expected service, but the standards and design may not be adequate. The service specification as used by the service provider differs from the expected service as *perceived* by the service provider. This is referred to as Gap 1 in service quality in the diagram above.

When some inadequate specifications of service management system, process, tools, functions etc. are designed, service providers use those specifications to produce the service. This is the source of Gap 2, as shown in the diagram above. Gap 2 is purely because the system failed within the service provider domain. When actual service delivery starts that is based on the designs and standards, the implementation and adoption of those standards and methodologies are transferred from an actual standard of design on paper. There is always a difference between what you intend to do and what you actually do, primarily because of imperfections in tools and inadequacy of training people. For example, say a customer was expecting 99.9% availability of service, but the system was not designed to serve that purpose—or, if the customer was expecting the issue to be resolved at the first call, but the service desk agent was not trained in the technology needed to resolve the issue.

Even if all the things went right till this point, the actual service delivered by the service provider may differ from the service expected by the user. The contract or SOW may not have any bearing on expectations. For example, say the SLA was three days to install the software; you designed your system and trained people to complete the installation in three days, but the customer was expecting installation in two days. This is an example of Gap 3, as shown in the diagram above. If the service provider does not do anything to set the customer's expectation, the expectation will be set by the customer.

Before, during, and after service rendering, there is regular communication between the service provider and the service receiver. Most often these are overstated and tall claims about the capabilities and feedbacks and do not match with actual service delivery. There are also external communications that are not usually authorized communications about the services: for example, the marketing campaign of competitors against the service provider. These communications influence the perception of the customer as well. Many times, service providers alter their designs to come in line with market trends. All these factors produce Gap 4, as shown in the diagram above.

The resultant sum of all the gaps is Gap 5 (as shown in the diagram above), and that gap stems from all false perceptions and expectations combined. Both perceptions and expectations are very difficult to measure and thus make perfection in the service industry seemingly impossible.

3.2.4 Gaps Originating from Outsourcing Service Contracts

in the previous sections, I talked about service-quality gaps and referred to the SOW as one source of gaps. Now I will explain the flaw that introduces the gap.

Remote Infrastructure Management (RIM) is a commonly outsourced service. Organizations are spending a lot of time, effort, and money to select the right outsourcing vendor and establish a contract. The customer requests that the managed-service provider provide complete IT infrastructure management, only because the customer has reached a situation where he alone cannot manage his IT efficiently and effectively. The most likely root cause is the customer's chaotic state of ITSM processes because of absence of ITSM architecture and processes because of absence of ITSM architecture and not because of low technical skills. Often business grows, but IT processes cannot scale up. Everyone does their own thing and ends up with different kinds of policies and procedures that lead to individual groups working independently in isolation without adequate collaboration (this structure is most commonly known as silos of towers in IT organization) and that explode costs. The customer chooses outsourcing to drive out these costs. Although there is an alternate option of cost reduction by improving the process and productivity, but that is not explored.

Typically, the error starts from the structure of Request for Proposal (RFP) and RFP response itself. An absolute clarity on vendors' roles about "managing technology" vs. "managing end to end service" is often missing. While the vendor's intent may be to go for managed service, RFP documents dictate the task-level requirements that customers want service providers to do. Ideally, in managed-service outsourcing, the customer should specify the results to be achieved (in terms of SLA) rather than tasks to be performed. Besides this, these tasks are usually an incomplete list and do not form the complete process. These tasks are more often listed for technology management and thus do not guarantee the production of the expected service and service levels. And the problem does not end here; there is another contradiction: the customer specifies, without any condition, both the task and the result. The fact is that the tasks do not produce results; it is the processes that produce the result. Therefore, if those tasks are not logically connected in a well-defined process, the desired result may not be achieved. Often managed-service providers undertake the services on an "as is" process basis. If customers' employees (despite good knowledge of their environment) could not manage their IT with their processes, how can vendors manage with the same processes and with less knowledge about their environment? Since the outsourcing service provider delivers the price advantage for executing tasks, the deal looks good on paper. However, soon these kinds of services turn out to be a "mess for less" proposition. This is a result of mixing responsibility with accountability—or, rather, not differentiating them in the context of task and process. The same fault is repeated, but the customer changes at each occasion. This reminds me of Albert Einstein's definition of insanity: "doing same thing again and again and expecting a different result."

In my view, if it is task outsourcing, then the vendor is responsible for deliverables, and the customer remains accountable for the result. In other words, it is the process that defines outcomes; therefore, the owner of process would always be accountable.

There are several things that the customer wrongly expects from an outsourced vendor. Frequently referred-to expectations are around transformation and value addition that we have discussed in this book's introduction. Yet another expectation is around thought leadership. Where is the scope of thought leadership in task outsourcing?

There are a lot of sourcing advisory and consulting companies who are paid hefty fees by customers who are seeking to outsource their IT infrastructure management and/or application management. These consulting companies are experts in guiding and managing the vendor selection process using their methods but still fail to differentiate between technology management and service management. In fact, they repeat the same faulty concept of dictating the tasks but expecting the result.

3.2.5 Processes to Close the Gaps

Let's relook at *Figure 23: Service quality gap model* - Gap 0 is the foundation of all the gaps, even though the Gap 5 is the result of all gaps and occurs because of one of the most intangible factor for measurement: perception. Preparation of SOW/contracts is usually dominated by legal professionals who are not the actual users or deliverer of services, and, if the stronger participation does not come from the service provider and consumer, there will always be a risk of setting a foundation of future gaps. Since customers drive SOW, and the contracts are driven by the customers, customers unknowingly set up the foundation of service-quality gaps.

By translating customer-service expectations into clear service agreements, Gap 1 can be closed. In ITSM process terminology, you will need strong service-design processes, especially service-catalog management, service-level management, capacity management, and availability management.
Once a comprehensive service agreement is in place, proceed toward using that agreement as a basis for planning and implementing the service delivery. In an ITIL context, this is the service transition process: namely, service asset and configuration management, service validation, and testing and evaluation. Next, ensure that service delivery and support is done according to planning and procedures. These plans and procedures are covered in the ITIL service operation process set. Finally, manage the configuration about the service delivery via a governance process to close Gap 4. These processes are included in the service strategy and the continual service improvement process (CSIP) of ITIL.

3.2.6 Customers' Role in SLA achievement

A customer has a vital role to play in the SLA being achieved. We have already looked at the benefits of an SLA and how it creates two-way accounting. There is two-way accountability to provide information and participate; if the user doesn't meet their obligation, the end service and user experience will be likely be poor. We have also talked about the RACI for SLAs, where someone will be accountable, responsible, consulted and informed. It is quite possible that the customer themselves will be playing one or more of these roles in the RACI.

3.3 SLA publishing

The SLA should be published in a service catalog, ideally where it is easily accessible by users. Once of the critical success criteria for SLAs to be clearly communicated to end users. The most logical place for this could be the self-service portal where users go to request for services.

The service catalogue is a listing of Live services provided and supported by IT. Each "service" could contain additional consumable components' or "service requests". Each "Service" could be a "business service" (e.g. Email) or an "IT service" (e.g. computing) that could be used to support other services. Each "Service" will likely contain 'consumable components' or "Service Requests", which may require approvals, be available to all or restricted. For example, the "Email" service, may contain 'Service requests" for:

- A new mailbox with 500 MB (available to all)
- A new mailbox with 1 GB (restricted to managers only)
- Creation of a new Distribution List

Any catalog must clearly communicate what the user will receive from the service – the deliverable; this is very important. It should also be written in a non-technical language that is easy for people to read and understand. Typical information that is published on the catalog for each service are listed below:

Service Name	The agreed name for the service.
Service Description	A brief description of what the service does, and the expected outcomes.
Features	Briefly outline the main features and functionalities of the service.
Service Category	Classify the service into one of the categories previously agreed. Categories are important to provide the Service Catalogue with a hierarchical view of services.

Service Type	Customer-facing service or supporting service. A customer-facing service is an IT service that is visible to end users or the business. Typical data to be recorded are those connecting to the business, although information from the supporting layer can be recorded as well for internal use by IT.A supporting service is an IT service that is not directly used by the business but is required by to deliver customer facing services (for example, a directory service or a backup service). Supporting services may also include IT services only used by IT (e.g. monitoring).
Service Owner(s)	Name and contact information of the person(s) with this role.
Business Owner(s)	Name and contact information of the person(s) with this role.
IT Owner	Name and contact information of the person(s) with this role.
VMO contact	Name and contact information of the person(s) responsible for managing the contract and relationship with the external provider(s) for this service
Service Provider(s)	Name and contact information of the providers who provide/support this service

Business Unit(s)	Business unit(s) to which the service is provided
Business Impact	Describe the positive impact of having the service available and/or the negative impact of the opposite. The impact can be quantified by the number of users affected, the impact on each user, and the cost to the business.
Business Priority	Select from a previously agreed scale like Critical/None-critical or High/Medium/Low.
Business Contacts	Name and contact information of the key business person(s) to be contacted in each region
Service Level Agreement (SLA)	Fulfilment times. A link to the document with the SLA encompassing the IT service can also be provided.
Service Hours	Write here the agreed time period when the IT service should be available.
Escalation Contacts	Name and contact information of the person(s) to be contacted when an escalation procedure is triggered.
Service Reports	A list of the operational reports required / available for the service.
Service Reviews	Frequency of the service level review meetings.

Request Procedures	Describe how the service should be requested (to be used to build and link to Service Requests)
Pricing and Chargeback	Establish how customers are charged.
Policies	Describe any policies governing the use of the service.
Supporting Services	List any supporting services on which the IT service depends.
Services Supported	List any service this service is supporting.

Table 4: Typical information published on a catalog per service

3.3.1 Why you need to publish SLAs

The core purpose of publishing the SLA is to set the right expectations. If you do not set the users expectation, then they will set one for themselves. Once the SLA is documented, set clear criteria, then communicating and setting the expectations of users should be a lot easier. I have come across several customers, where users have been complaining of a poor service; however, on looking at the performance reports of the suppliers, they were all being achieved. The perceived service was poor, because the expectations of the user had never been set, so matter how good a service the provider delivered, the user was always disappointed.

3.3.2 Why the portfolio and catalog are important for SLAs

The portfolio and catalog are important, as they clearly list what services you offer. The difference between the portfolio and catalog is that the portfolio also lists services that are in the pipeline (forthcoming) and ones that have been decommissioned. Whereas, the catalog only lists live services. If you have got the portfolio and catalog, then you already have a list of defined services, which becomes the foundation and the platform for also publishing and communicating the SLA. If, however you don't have a catalog and you cannot clearly articulate what you offer, how will you set expectations of what you will deliver?

3.4 Managing SLAs

The data points required to measure the SLA should be clear and provisions made in the ITSM tool and/or other systems to be able to capture the data required for calculating the SLA. A data source must exist for computing the SLA achievement. SLAs should never be measured on any manually entered data. I had a client in 2004, where a supplier provided onsite support for end user devices. The client insisted on an SLA for how quickly the field resource arrived onsite. There was no way to know when this was done, unless the support resource said when he arrived, no system existed that could generate this timestamp. He was asked to enter this manually, which basically was a guarantee that the SLAs would be met. Integrity of data cannot be guaranteed by manual data entry.

3.4.1 Monitoring

The SLM module in the tool is basically the monitoring of the SLA. It is also supported by notifications. The notifications themselves can defeat the purpose. Sending notifications at every stage of progression ending up bombarding the user's mailbox. With hundreds of notifications, the most common approach for IT support staff is to put a rule to put these notifications into a separate folder, which they never read. So, the notifications serve no purpose at all.

Vendors call it a Service Level Management module, when it actually is restricted to only measuring and monitoring the progress of the agreed levels, not management of the service levels. Clients who buy this thinking they are buying a service level management processes are even more delusional.

3.4.2 Measuring and reporting

"Everything cannot be measured objectively" is a teaching from the Dalai Lama. But any agreed SLAs and KPIs must be measured, tracked and reported. The measurement methodology must be agreed, data sources identified, but also the format and method that the SLA will be reported and published should also be agreed with the customer. There are several reporting tools and dashboards available in the market. Most ITSM tools also provide the capability natively, although the usually only work on the data available within the ITSM system, rather than aggregating data from multiple sources. SLA reporting dashboards enable you to easily view how well you are meeting your SLA policies. This dashboard breaks down your SLA metrics by policy, time, and status, so you can identify problem areas. Analytics tools aggregate data from multiple sources. They can even work on unstructured data. Do not make your ITSM tool as the reporting tool with the addition of multiple custom fields.

Ideally, your reporting solution should provide some mechanism to generate and look at trends, compare performance between reporting periods or even drill down into actual ticket or even details.

3.4.3 Improving SLAs vs improving the service

SLAs are fundamental to effectively measuring the performance of the service. They also provide the basis for managing the relationship between the service provider and the customer. Basically, SLAs are intended to ensure the provider understands what they are supposed to deliver, the customer knows what to expect, and both can see what is actually being delivered.

Does improving the SLA automatically improve the service being delivered? It may be true, but not always. It will depend entirely on the SLA and the way it is defined and measured. I had already provided an example of FCR and average call handling times as two SLAs, which when combined but not defined correctly could actually provide a negative service due to the way it would drive the suppliers behavior *(see section 2.1.4).*

Both aspects need to be looked at objectively; the requirements should be revisited and then based on real evidence and data, a decision should be made on either improving the SLA due to poor performance, or improving the service or even both. There may also be a requirement to change, drop or add an SLA!

3.5 Where SLAs fail?

There are several common reasons why SLAs fail, let's look at some.

- Fuzzy expectation
- Unrealistic expectation
- Realistic expectation
- Implicit expectation
- Explicit expectation

Fuzzy expectations exist when customers expect a service provider to solve a problem or provide something as a part of the service but do not have a clear understanding of what should be done or what is that part.

Explicit expectations are clear in the customer's minds in advance of the service process, although those may or may not be understood by the service provider. Explicit expectation can be divided into realistic and unrealistic expectations.

Implicit expectations refer to element of a service which are so obvious to customers that they do not consciously think about them but take them for granted.

Customers normally presume that explicit expectations will be met, and unrealistic expectations might be exited. Service providers have to help customers adjust these unrealistic expectations into more realistic ones to ensure that a service delivery will meet customer expectations. In this stage, service providers should be aware of the vaguer promise or "implied" promise because it can form unrealistic explicit expectations that lead customers to believe that services offered will include features that in fact are not included. Beside explicit expectations, implicit expectations also have to be fulfilled because they are apparent that customers are clearly expressed. Such implicit services will become explicit if they are not fulfilled.

Perception management

Process of maintaining the perception at par with the expectation

A pre-requisite for this process to be applicable is expectation management is in place

This approach involves continuous testing of performance against the expectation and needs without any formal agreement. This process is based on the measurement of performance and perception and can be sketched as below

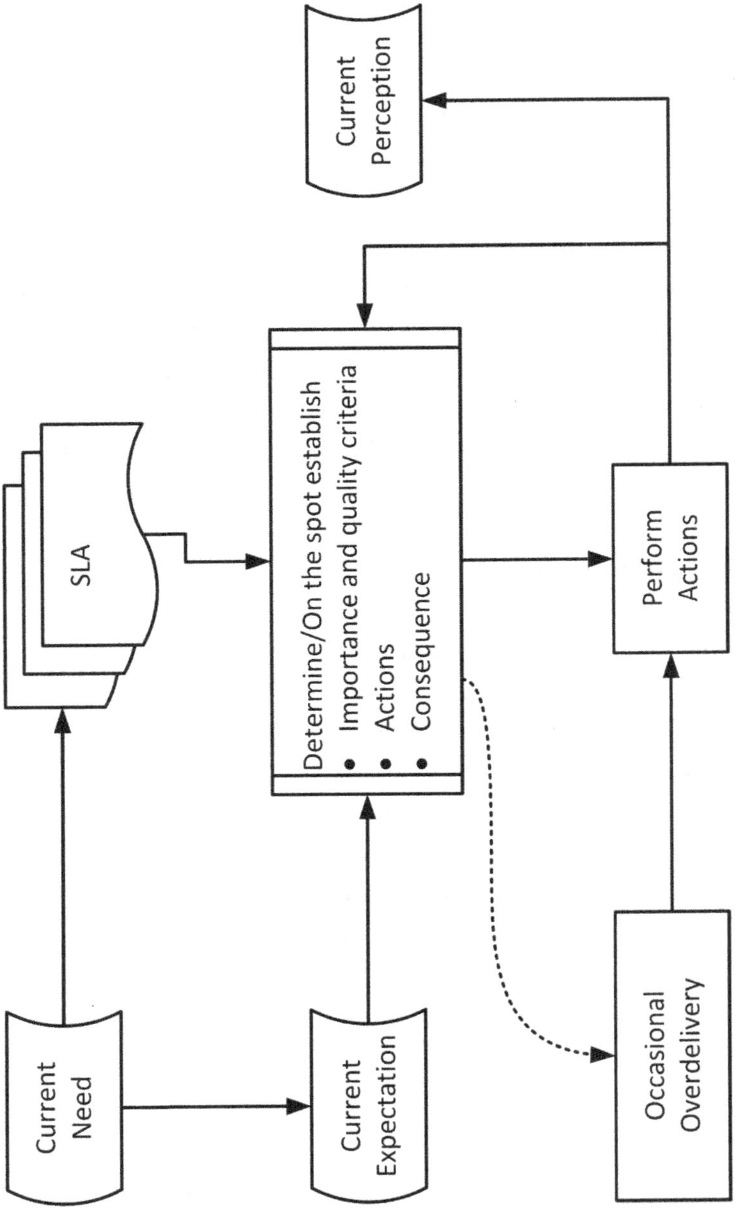

Figure 24: Perception Management

Another tool used by organizations to better get details or a customer's satisfaction or even perception is Net Promoter or Net Promoter Score (NPS). It can be used to gauge the loyalty of a firm's customer relationships. It serves as an alternative to traditional customer satisfaction research and claims to be correlated with revenue growth. I am not sure how it would work in a multi supplier environment, because when the user answers the one question *"How likely is it that you would recommend our company/product/service to a friend or colleague?"*, at the backend, the service is broken up into multiple parts, each provided by a different firm. So, it would end up being a reflection of the enterprise IT service. But do end users really have a choice of not using corporate IT services?

NPS is measured between -100 to +100. Anyone below 0 is a detractor, while everyone over 0 is a promoter. Scores can be as low as −100 (everybody is a detractor) or as high as +100 (everybody is a promoter). An NPS that is positive (i.e., higher than zero) is felt to be good, and an NPS of +50 is excellent

Empowerment of the delivery manager

This approach takes advantage of the fact that a customer is more readily prepared to criticize the bad service than to appreciate good service. While the above sketch is self-explanatory, it is important to understand that the success requires customer to be a part of service provider organization- a stronger bond than the traditional partnership. In simplest term, it is the successive elimination of high nuisance factors against quality based on customer perception in each iteration of actions. Prerequisites are:

- Customer and service provider should have sense of respect and equality. An attempt to dominate will ensure failure.
- Consensus culture should prevail in the parties
- Understanding each other's point of view is very important

Even over delivery of services has certain principles:

- Should be occasional, but shouldn't become the norm
- If it is delivered all the time, you shift the expectation of the user. The next time you do not over deliver, they will complain of a poor service even if it is within the contracted SLA. Look at how it works in the airline industry. Airlines do not upgrade passengers all the time or even when you want it, you get it when they want it. The airline decides whom to upgrade and when to upgrade. They have certain rules built in system and some are discretion of agent on the gate

Expectation vs Perception

Customer expectation is what the customer expects according to communicated SLAs (if not communicated, they will set their own expectation, which may be unrealistic), available resources and is influenced by experience with similar services and information available online. Customer perception is totally subjective and is based on the customer's interaction with the product or service. Perception is derived from the customer's satisfaction of the specific product or service and the quality of service delivery. In an ideal world the customer's expectation would be almost identical to the customer's perception. Expectation is before consumption of the service and perception is after consumption of the services.

Expectation Management

Isn't just doing a good job, good enough? The reality is that a good job is often subjective and doing a good job depends on what the recipient was expecting. One way to improve your effectiveness and deliver on expectations is to proactively manage expectations more effectively. The better you can manage the expectations, the higher the satisfaction will be of the user. The process of converting fuzzy expectation into explicit and realistic expectations is expectation management.

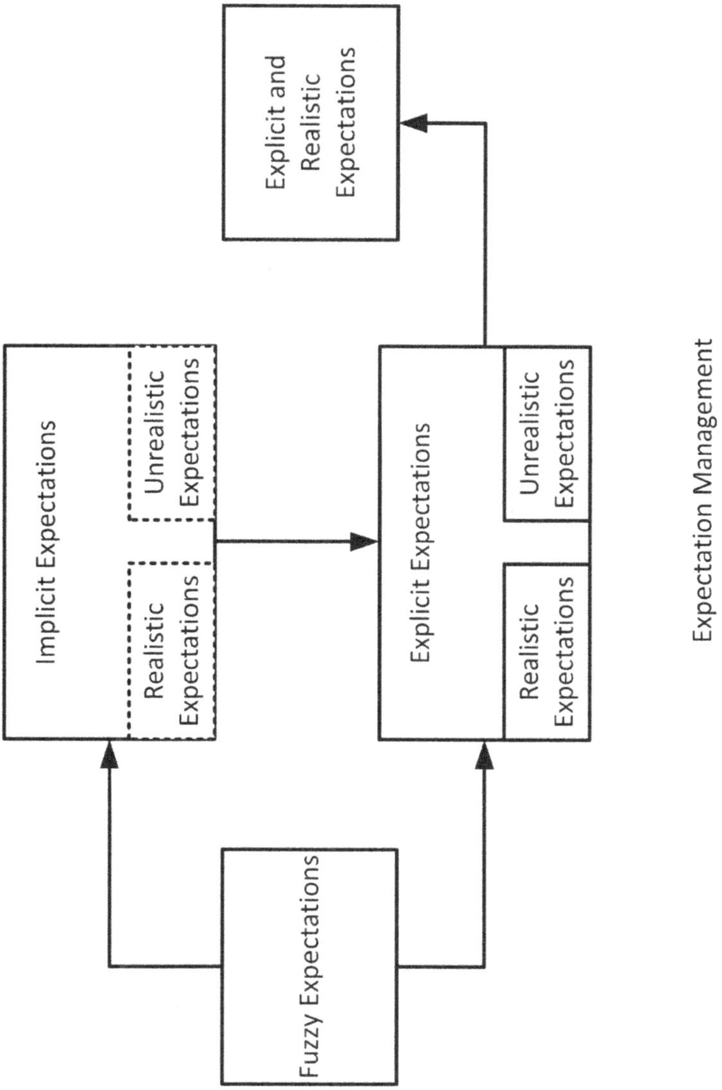

Figure 25: Expectation Management

The activities below depict the process steps of expectation management:

- Identify/discover implicit expectations
- Convert them to explicit
- Analyze explicit expectations
- Identify unrealistic
- Convert to realistic

I agree with the point that managing expectations is key to success. While under promising and over delivering is a good rule of thumb, the risk is you underwhelm people and lose their support. The best method to managing expectations is working in collaboration, with a clear mutual understanding, trust, transparency and open mindedness.

SLA influences Customer satisfaction

SLAs when communicated, establish the ground for explicit and realistic expectations. SLAs are the primary tool for converting fuzzy expectation

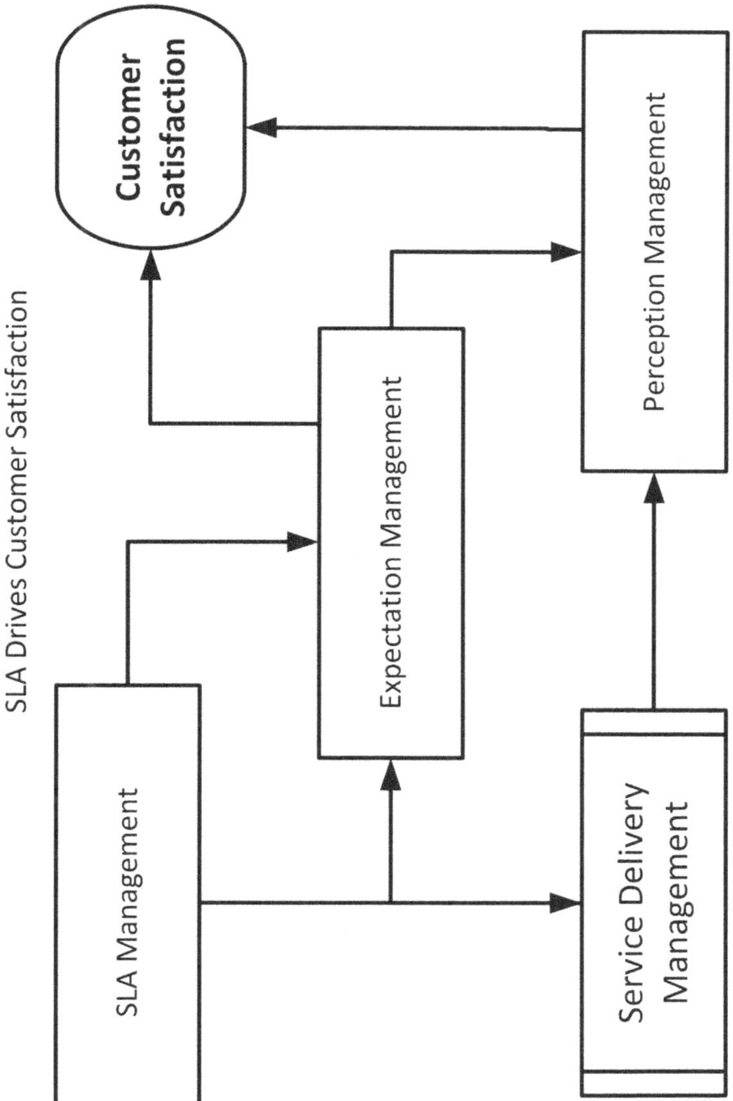

Figure 26: SLA Drives and influences Satisfaction

4 SLA gap analysis

Isn't it strange that the biggest criteria of good service, high availability and a fantastic user experience, i.e. the architecture and design – are not measured in outsourcing contracts?

Services have to be designed to achieve an agreed SLA. A higher availability SLA will require redundancy built into the architecture or the load balanced to achieve a performance target. In several outsourcing contracts, the approach is to validate if the target SLA has been historically achieved or not. You may have achieved it in the past "by the grace of god", but that does not guarantee that the new supplier will continue to achieve it as your infrastructure ages. There is rarely any consideration of the right architecture and the design of the service, neither is there any measurement for this, when it is actually fundamental to achieving any SLAs that you will agree for the output.

4.1 Gap analysis approach

The diagram below depicts the flow and steps to be taken when analyzing the gaps in SLAs. It is not that the target is not defined, it could be that other criteria required for the SLA to be achieved, measured or reported are missing.

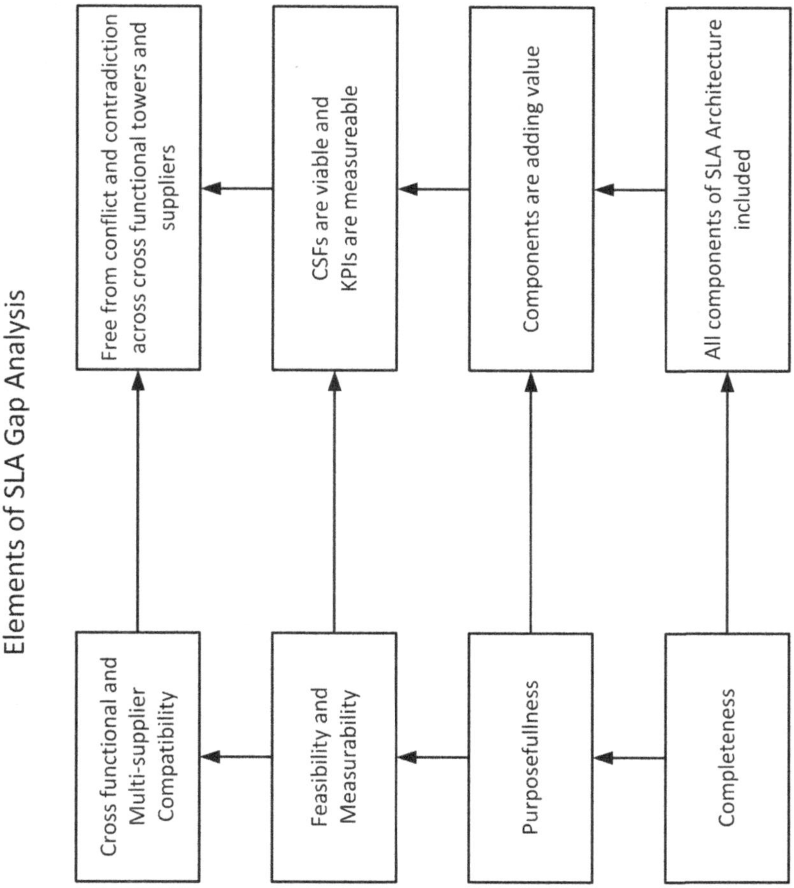

Figure 27: Gap analysis

- To gauge the completeness of the SLA, refer to the architecture diagram *(Figure 21: SLA Architecture)*; if all the factors have been designed and covered, then it can be considered as complete.
- To gauge the purposefulness of the SLA – refer to *Figure 22: Complexity versus Purposefulness of SLA* ; the more complex it get, the lesser it will be purposeful.
- To gauge the ability to measure, be clear on what you are measuring, your process should be generating the data required for measurements. Outcome based SLAs sound attractive; but can it be achieved? Task and output are easy to measure, outcome/result is a lot harder; refer to section *2.3.2 SLA for task vs SLA for results*

4.2 What will gap analysis do?

Performing a gap analysis is important to measure actual performance against targets and eventually to uncover hidden errors and issued. A gap analysis can give decision makers a comprehensive overview of the entire service and its performance allowing decision makers to determine whether the resources exist to meet their agreed targets for the services they offer. It will also allow you to realign your priorities and focusing on the purpose and possibly even simplifying the SLA and reducing complications (complexity may still be required to serve the business needs). The analysis will also likely assist you with saving costs, especially if you have been paying penalties due to breaching of agreed SLAs.

After an analysis, you may or may not have all the resources to address all the gaps. The gaps can be prioritized as high, medium and low; the classification does not necessarily mean the priority has ranking over others for attention or resources but may help when conducting further investigation into issues.

4.2.1 Generally observed Gaps:

- One sided SLAs

  A balanced SLA should provide a platform for both parties to have a successful and mutually beneficial relationship, it is not intended to favor one side only. There needs to be well defined and agreed incentives to improve as well as resolve issues when they do occur. Otherwise, there is always a risk that a supplier will ignore higher impact issues, only to deal with less critical ones just to avoid penalties. We had provided an example of FCR earlier in the book and the various interpretations and possibilities. In that example, there was no benefit for a supplier to put in automation tools to support password resets, so the benefit was all tipped to one side only.

- Incomplete RACI

  There are responsibilities and accountability on both sides for an SLA to be met. For a car to function as designed, the driver has to fulfil their duties and drive it well or fill the right type of fuel . Even a simple SLA of "delivering a set of reports" requires ownership on the client side to receive the reports, analyze and accept them. It is definitely a two way street.

- KPI, but no CSF

  It is common to find a laundry list of KPIs in an outsourcing contract. KPI's do not typically attract penalties, due to which, we have observed that they many a time do not get the level of attention that they should. There is no consequence of breaching them, apart from probably a slap on the wrist. But more importantly, because there is no financial penalty, the criteria that needs to be in place for them even to be met are completely ignored as the just don't receive the dame level of focus. After all, isn't it all to do with return on investment?

- Rationalization of multi supplier
  In a multi supplier ecosystem, contracts usually get negotiated at different times, unless you are a startup or doing through a de-merger. Most of the large organizations are not in this scenario. Each suppliers contract is negotiated based on the trend, technology and best available service at that time. Unfortunately, several months or years later, when new contracts are negotiated, the goalposts, requirements and level of service demanded is much higher. But due to the dependencies of the various components in a service chain, the suppliers too have a dependency on each other. And if everyone is playing with the goalpost in a different corner of the pitch, then it isn't really a team sport! I have come across scenarios where the priority one resolution target for the infrastructure provider was 2 hours, whereas the application providers was 4 hours, with completely different support hours – infrastructure was 24/7, while the application provider was 12x5. Now, when a service outage does occur, you need everyone on board working towards the same target, not one saying their resources aren't available as their contracts don't cater for support within certain timelines.

- "The cliff edge" - the maximum acceptable breach!
  Let me explain this with an example. Imagine a supplier is delivering several services to a client, this is not out of the ordinary. It is very common with application services providers. Not all applications are core or critical to the business, it is usually a handful. So it is common, to set a heavier penalty for the core services and less for the others (could also be referred to as "gold, silver, bronze" service). It is also quite common to have an elapsed time after the SLA breaches before the penalty is applied (i.e a threshold) and another target beyond which a higher or more significant penalty is applied (maximum threshold). The other, less important, applications have smaller degrees of penalty.
  So, if it happens to be a bad month and the critical service SLA has breached and the full penalty is applicable, then a rational "business"

decision on the supplier side could be to drop any additional efforts to restore the critical service and concentrate on those that can still affect his penalties.

- No benchmarks
  If you do not base the SLA on what is achievable, then you are only limited by your imaginations! But that wouldn't be reality, it would be a dream world. Clients have known to ask for 100% availability! Practically, this is clearly unachievable (unless ofcourse you put redundancy at every layer, followed by redundancy to cover the redundancy!). There is always a likelihood, no matter how small that at times things may go wrong, hardware may fail or the service may stop for reasons beyond your control. But even if we ignore a 100% target, suppliers have known to agree to unrealistic SLAs with no information on what the current performance achievements are. If the technology, architecture, way of working stays the same, then the reality is that the SLA will not improve. It may be a case of "my mess for less", but not better SLAs.

- No ability to measure
  If you can't measure it, then you can't manage it. SLAs that can't be measured serve no purpose as a supplier will never breach them, neither can you really assess how the service is. It is not just a technology issue (i.e we do not have the technology to measure it). Several times, the definition of a service itself will mean that you are unable to measure it. In a recent client engagement, I noticed that one of the suppliers had been asked to agree to an SLA in case there were any audits. Sensible requirement. But, the SLA stated *"Timely response for audits - Respect of time for providing information in case of an Audit"*. How can you possibly measure this?

- Caveats and get out clauses

  Yes, you do need to cater for the unforeseen, but it needs to be sensible. To give you another example, a couple of years ago, I was involved in the negotiation to sign a contract for a new software service provider. With cloud based software, the core SLA you typically look at is "availability". The SLA stated – *"Supplier shall, during the purchased term of any agreement for Software Services, make such Software Services available 24 hours a day, seven days a week with an availability of 99.7% on a monthly basis except for:*

  - planned, pre-announced scheduled maintenance.

  - unscheduled emergency maintenance upto 10 hours a month

  Can you really agree to a supplier having "unscheduled emergency maintenance" subtracted from an availability SLA? By incorporating this, the actual availability SLA is not 99.7%, but instead 98.3%, which equates to a little over 12 hours of downtime per month. Imagine your core business being down for half a day three times a week, surely that wouldn't be acceptable?

I cannot stress on the importance of a SLA being designed correctly, with not only the right expertise and a clear understanding of what is realistically achievable, but also makes business sense. It is very easy for clients to ask for the impossible and for suppliers to agree and make commitments that cannot be met. It is even easier to agree to incorrectly designed SLAs that eventually lead to a broken down relationship. You only learn from bad experience. We hope you will gain some learnings and insights from our experiences to help you design more sensible SLAs.

About the authors

Prafull Verma

Prafull Verma has a bachelor's degree in electronics and communication engineering and has over thirty years' experience in the area of electronic data processing and information technology. He started his career in India in the area of electronic data processing systems and later moved to the United States in 1997. During the past thirty years, he has worked on diversified areas in computer science and information technologies. Some of his key experience areas are the design and implementation of heterogeneous networks, midrange technical support management, end-user service management and design, and the implementation and management of process-driven ITSM systems.

Prafull has acquired a unique blend of expertise in integrated areas of tools, process, governance, operations, and technology. He is the author of several methodology and frameworks for IT service management that include multi- vendor ITIL frameworks, ITSM for cloud computing and Service Integration.

Prafull's competencies and specializations include the area of merging engineering with service management, as this book manifests, and outsourcing business management.

Currently, Prafull is working for HCL Technologies Ltd. DRYiCE LOB, as Fellow and Chief Architect. In recent past he was also a member of the product advisory council of ServiceNow, the industry leading ITSM platform for four years in a row.

About the authors

Mohan Kewalramani

Mohan Kewalramani has over 18 years of experience in IT service management transformation projects, ITIL consultancy, process re-engineering and ITSM tool deployments.

Mohan spent the early years of his professional career in the Middle East, before moving to the UK in 2007 and has worked with customers all over the Middle East, Europe and the USA. His knowledge goes beyond the theoretical and he prides himself on having implemented the realistic, practical and efficient, including implementations in multi-supplier environments with cross delivery processes, interfaces, including tools and technology to support service and systems management and has led large service management projects, with varying degrees of complexity including several in a multi supplier outsourcing environment.

Mohan is employed with HCL Technologies Ltd., Infrastructure Service Division, and DRYiCE Business Unit, as Director and Global Head of the Service Integration and Management Practice.

About the authors

Kalyan Kumar

Kalyan Kumar (KK) is the Chief Technologist for HCL Technologies – ISD and leads all the Global Technology Practices. In his current role Kalyan is responsible defining Architecture & Technology Strategy, New Solutions Development & Engineering across all Enterprise Infrastructure, Business Productivity, Unified Communication Collaboration & Enterprise Platform/DevOps Service Lines. Kalyan is also responsible for Business and Service Delivery for Cross Functional Services for HCL across all service lines globally.

Kalyan is widely acknowledged as an expert and path-breaker on BSM/ITSM & IT Architecture and Cloud Platforms and has developed many IPs for the company in these domains. He is also credited with building HCL MTaaSTM Service from the scratch, which has a multi-million turnover today and a proprietary benchmark for Global IT Infrastructure Services Delivery. His team is also credited with developing the MyCloudSM platform for Cloud Service Management & MyDevOps, which is a pioneering breakthrough in the Utility Computing and Hybrid Agile Ops Model space. He has been presented with many internal and industry awards for his thought leadership in the IT Management space.

Kalyan also runs the HCL ISD IPDEV Incubator Group where he is responsible for incubating new services, platforms and IPs for the company. He is also active in the Digital Systems Integration Roadmap and Solutions Strategy for HCL.

Kalyan has spoken at many prestigious industry platforms and is currently actively engaged in Partner Advisory Board of CA Technologies, IBM Software etc.

In his free time Kalyan likes to jam with his band Contraband as a drummer / percussionist and reviews Consumer Technology Gadgets and follows Cricket Games Diligently. Kalyan lives in New Delhi, India with his family.

KK can be followed on Twitter @KKLIVE and at Linkedin (http://www.linkedin. com/in/kalyankumar).

From the same Authors

Process Excellence for IT Operations: a Practical Guide for IT Service Process Management

Authored by Mr Prafull Verma, Authored by Mr Kalyan Kumar B

List Price: $29.95
6" x 9" (15.24 x 22.86 cm)
Black & White on White paper
332 pages
Process Excellence for IT Operations
ISBN-13: 978-0615877525 (Custom Universal)
ISBN-10: 0615877524
BISAC: Computers / Information Technology

As the title suggests, the book is providing a practical guidance on managing the processes for IT Services. There are lot of guidance available on technology management in IT industry but this book is focusing on technology independent service management. The book will be addressed to all IT people from a process practitioner perspective, however, the fundamentals are presented in simplistic terms, and therefore it should be useful to all IT people. It will describe the process engineering concept and how it can be applied to IT Service Management. This is not about the industry standard framework such as ITIL and COBIT but about the common processes that are generally used in real life operations. This book does not focus on any technology.

Foundation of IT Operations Management: Event Monitoring and Controls

Authored by Mr Prafull Verma, Authored by Mr Kalyan Kumar B

List Price: $15.95
6" x 9" (15.24 x 22.86 cm)
Black & White on White paper
138 pages
Foundation Of IT Operation
ISBN-13: 978-0692205709
(Custom Universal)
ISBN-10: 0692205705
BISAC: Computers /
Information Technology

In IT operations, event monitoring and control - where you continuously monitor the health of IT infrastructure and take proactive measures to prevent the interruptions in IT services- is dominated by tools and technology but there is a meticulous process behind it. This book tries to demystify the underlying process for this kind of operation management. There are lot many books on service management but those books do not cover this subject adequately and leave this area to be addressed by tools and technology. Tools vendor on the other hand, focus on the tool part, leaving the process aspect to the service management professionals. This book fills in the void and connects both, the process and the tools to provide a holistic view. The book takes an educative tone and written primarily for IT generalist and not for the tool experts, although it would give a new perspective to tool experts also.

Service Integration: A Practical Guide to Multivendor Service Management

Authored by Mr Prafull Verma, Authored by Mr Kalyan Kumar B

List Price: $15.95
6" x 9" (15.24 x 22.86 cm)
Black & White on White paper
138 pages
Foundation Of IT Operation
ISBN-13: 978-0692205709
(Custom Universal)
ISBN-10: 0692205705
BISAC: Computers / Information Technology

This book is intended to present simplified guide for IT generalists who are new to the service integration subject. The purpose of this book is to educate all IT professionals with the basic concepts of the service integration. Additionally the purpose is to provide the core guidance and foundation guidance to Service Management professionals, upon which they can build and implement the service integration in their environment.

Software Asset Management: Understanding and implementing an optimal solution

Authored by Mr Prafull Verma, Authored by Mr Kalyan Kumar B

List Price: $15.95
6" x 9" (15.24 x 22.86 cm)
Black & White on White paper
148 pages
Software Asset Management
ISBN-13: 978-0692324264
(Custom Universal)
ISBN-10: 0692324267
BISAC: Computers / Information Technology

Software asset management (SAM) is an essential need for all IT organizations, not just because of the cost of software but also because of the potential litigation of copyright violation for use of unlicensed software. Most of the organizations deploy tools for software asset management, but fail to achieve the desired goals because tools are a small part of the holistic solution. This books explains the underlying complexity of SAM and includes all aspects of SAM solution that includes solution architecture, the SAM processes, tools and function and provide a guideline to develop, build and operate an optimal solution

Foundation of Intelligent IT Operations: CMDB and Service Maps

Authored by Mr. Prafull Verma, Authored by Mr. Mohan Kewalramani, Authored by Mr. Kalyan Kumar

List Price: $15.95
6" x 9" (15.24 x 22.86 cm)
Black & White on White paper
172 pages
Software Asset Management
ISBN-13: 978-0692380925
(Custom Universal)
ISBN-10: 0692380922
BISAC: Computers /
Information Technology

The scale of enterprise IT environments are growing rapidly and computing resources are deployed in abundance. Consequently, management of IT operations gets increasingly complex. Service Maps and the CMDB (Configuration Management Database) are key tools to enable an organization to intelligently manage the complexity of dependencies and relationships between components. Theoretically, this sounds reasonable and easily achievable, especially since the concept of a CMDB was introduced in ITIL v2 more than a decade ago and the assumption is that almost all organizations that have adopted ITIL would have a CMDB and be delivering on its intended objectives. The reality is far removed from theory though.

Designing, implementing and maintaining a sensible CMDB that is fit for purpose and does not end up being a project set up for failure requires more than just theoretical knowledge. Additionally, with the rapid adoption of cloud computing, Internet of Things (IoT) and other disruptive technologies in an increasingly complex multi supplier environment with implementations of "Service Integration and Management (SIAM)", the old school vision of the CMDB needs to be designed with a renewed perspective to keep it relevant to our IT environments today.

This book tries to educate IT generalists with the basics of a CMDB and service maps without the need for understanding technology or any specialist tools, while trying to guide IT service management professionals to build an intelligent information system that produces real benefits to support the management of IT services by having a reliable and enriched source of information, that helps in making better, more informed decisions.

Foundation for XaaS: Service Architecture in 21st Century Enterprise

Authored by Prafull Verma, Authored by Kalyan Kumar

List Price: $12.95
6" x 9" (15.24 x 22.86 cm)
Black & White on White paper
152 pages
Service Integration
ISBN-13: 978-0692688311
(Custom Universal)
ISBN-10: 0692688315
BISAC: Computers /
Information Technology

XaaS is a collective term said to stand for a number of things including "X as a service,". Everything (and anything!) as a service is a rapidly expanding model not only in Cloud service but also in every other industry. It grew from utility service model and applied to IT and now non-IT services as well. This is the new delivery models and shall warrant new approach to service management. But before that it will require a new approach to design and publish a service. Like service management architecture that we discussed in our earlier publication, service architecture is largely an ignored aspect in service design. IT professionals talk more about application architecture than the service architecture. This book discusses the sets of service properties that collectively form a service architecture and then also talks about the building blocks of XaaS service management system.

Epilogue

This is age of Service. Everything is Service and Service is everything ! Of all the characteristics of a Product, perhaps it is Service that matter most. Yes, the quality of the underlying product is very important but if poorly delivered and serviced, the quality will not matter. Sometimes perceptions also matter particularly in the area of customer satisfaction or customer delight. But for most routine, general purpose and daily matters, what matters most is Service and its measurement about how well it is delivered.

Perhaps a couple of decades back, many things were taken for granted and also not that well explored, so the service measurements and awareness about Service Level Agreements have evolved in these years. But now we are almost at a very mature level within some parts of the Industry/Business but at the same time there is gross lack of awareness about the very concepts of SLAs. While many business deals are negotiated around SLAs, the end-user is faintly aware of them and there seem to be no concerted effort to increase this awareness in an all-round manner.

Prafull has been dabbling with this field for over a decade now and it is very appropriate that such treatise of this subject comes from him as sequel to his other work which is mainly around Services. Given the fact that most business run on IT or depend on IT in modern times, it is not out of place to have IT in the backdrop for many concepts around Services and associated SLAs. Although there is no explicit mention of IT or assumption about some services being delivered through IT, I suppose most readers who have experienced IT in the background of most services that they avail from within the enterprise or from outside like travel or hospitality industry, etc.

Hopefully some readers will leverage information and ideas provided in this book and develop their own Framework of SLAs for the services they use, deliver, or deal with. New ideas and notions about SLAs should thus emerge in this manner to enrich this field which binds humans together through services of all kinds. Business, Governments, Societies, NGOs, and many entities dealing with public at large are actually dealing with Services at large, so this field is very important for all of us.

Prof. Kavindra Sharma
Visiting Faculty
Narsee Monjee Institute of Management Studies
Mumbai

Made in the USA
Monee, IL
04 November 2026

67382858R00105